Encyclopedia of Flags and Coats of Arms

Webster's
Concise Encyclopedia of
FLAGS
& COATS OF ARMS

Ludvík Mucha

Illustrations by Stanislav Valášek

Editor: William G. Crampton

CRESCENT BOOKS
New York

Translated by Jiří Louda and edited by William G. Crampton
Director of the Flag Institute, Chester
© Geodetic and Cartographic enterprise in Prague, 1985
All rights reserved.
First published in Great Britain by Orbis Publishing Limited,
London 1985.

Published in the United States of America 1985 by Crescent
Books, distributed by Crown Publishers, Inc.
Reprinted in 1987.

Library of Congress Cataloging in Publication Data
    Bibliography: p.
    1. Emblems, National. 2. Flags. I. Crampton,
W. G. (William G.) II. Title: Flags & coats of arms.
III. Title: Flags and coats of arms.
CR 191.W43 1985 929.9'2 85-19069
ISBN 0-517-499517

All rights reserved. No part of this publication may be re-
produced, stored in a retrieval system, or transmitted, in any
form or by any means, electronic, mechanical, photo-
copying, recording or otherwise, without the prior permission of the publishers. Such permission, if granted, is
subject to a fee depending on the nature of the use.

h g f e d c

Printed in Czechoslovakia

CONTENTS

Introduction

International flags and coats of arms generally attract people's attention at events such as exhibitions, military parades, the Olympic Games and other international sporting occasions. While some flags may be familiar, others often cannot be identified without further assistance. In such cases people might refer to a handbook or search in an encyclopedia or an atlas, but often their interest does not stop there. They begin perhaps to study the components of a coat of arms, or look for reasons why one particular flag is different from, or similar to, other flags. A country's flag and coat of arms represent its history, culture and political and social system as well as the national and aesthetic feelings of the designers. In addition, there is usually a close link between a country's flag and its coat of arms. The flag is often a coloured simplification of the arms, its colours sometimes reflecting those of the arms as well as having special symbolism suggesting national aspirations, the desired path of evolution or a specific political creed. These characteristics help us to understand the people, their ideals, their way of life and their perspectives on their social and political development.

This handbook is intended to help in the interpretation of these symbols and also to introduce the reader to the basic history and rules of "vexil - lology" — the young and still developing science concerned with flags. In the following pages, flags of all the independent and dependent countries of the world are illustrated and described, but only independent countries have their coats of arms depicted in full colour. Flag badges and emblems of some dependent territories, together with other interesting details of some of the arms appearing on flags, will be found in the text in black and white. All flags are illustrated in their correct proportions. Federated states (e.g. the USA, Federal Republic of Germany, Switzerland, Yugoslavia, Austria, Brazil, Malaysia and Australia) are represented only by the national flag of the federation since the inclusion of the flags of the component parts of these states would inevitably mean a disproportionate extension of the book.

The text is divided into seven sections, each representing a continent. Within each section the flags of independent and dependent countries are described separately in alphabetical order. A complete alphabetical list of all the countries of the world (regardless of whether they have their own flag or they use the flag of their mother country) is given at the end of the book.

The maps heading each section give in capital letters the names of all the countries which have their own flags, whether these countries are independent or not. The names of countries with no flag of their own have only an initial capital letter.

Flags and arms follow the flow of events — the old ones disappear to be replaced by new ones. New flags also appear when new independent nations are born. To keep abreast of these changes is not easy without access to one of the periodicals listed at the end of the book; one of these is "Flagmaster", published quarterly in Chester, England.

Flags

What is a flag? It is a piece of cloth, most often rectangular, with prescribed proportions (usually 2 : 3) which is fastened to, or hoisted from, a staff or mast by means of a halyard. Flags are categorized according to the purpose for which they are used; there are, for example, state flags, national flags, government flags, service flags, merchant flags, military flags, ensigns, city flags, signal flags and international flags. Originally there were no strictly prescribed proportions for flags and their components, and there were a number of early types from which modern flags have developed, e.g. vexillum, labarum, gonfanon, banner, standard, cornet and guidon. With the evolution of international law there soon followed a precise definition of flags, with precisely stipulated functions, and flags became binding symbols. Today they are one of the symbols of national sovereignty and play an important role in international relations.

Much older than flags were "vexilloids" which were symbols made of material other than cloth, but which functioned as flags and were displayed at the top of poles. Possibly the oldest are the vexilloid provincial standards from Egypt pictured on a slate stele of the pharaoh Narmer of the 1st dynasty (2900 BC), now kept in Cairo. Somewhat younger, dating from the end of the third millennium BC, is a metallic Iranian vexilloid, probably the oldest standard still in existence. It was found by an archaeological expedition in the ruins of the ancient city of Khablis. Other documents from the pre-vexillological period come from the regions of Mesopotamian and Indian culture (2500–2000 BC). The Greek civilization held the prime position in Europe in the use of standards on ships. An example of this sort is the "phoinikis" (the name suggests that the custom was taken over from the Phoenicians), a piece of a purple-coloured garment which is said to have been used by the Greek commander Themistocles in the sea battle at the island of Salamis in 480 BC as a signal for the Greek navy to attack the Persians. In the 3rd and 4th centuries BC Roman troops used the so-called Dragon Standard taken over from the Dacians. This was a hollow tube fastened at the top of a staff, which, when air flowed through it, took on the shape of a dragon. The mysterious Raven Flag of the Vikings, appearing for the first time in AD 878 and hoisted by Leif Ericsson in about AD 1000 during his famous voyage to North America, was perhaps constructed in a similar way.

Top left: Early Chinese "flag" from the Wu Liang shrine
Top right: Roman Vexillum
Above left: Labarum of Constantine the Great
Above: Gonfanon
Left: Raven Flag of the Vikings

Banner

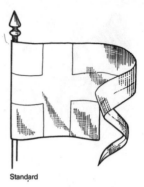

Standard

The first flags as we know them today, made of cloth, appeared in China. They may have developed from ribbons which had originally been a decorative part of the vexilloids. Legend has it that at the time of the Chou conquest (in the second half of the 12th century BC) a white war flag was carried before King Wu, founder of the Chou dynasty. China developed a system of flag types which is evidenced by pictures of these symbols on the Wu Liang shrine (Han dynasty: 206 BC to AD 220) in Shantung province; they were very similar to present-day flags in that they appear to be of cloth and are fastened to a pole. The oldest existing silk banner, in the shape of the letter T, was found in 1972 in the ancient burial ground in Ma-wang-tui near Ch'angsha in Hunan province and comes from the 2nd century BC.

The first flag of the Western world was the Roman "vexillum" introduced in 105 BC by Consul Gaius Marius as a distinguishing sign for the Roman legions. It was a piece of cloth, usually purple or red but sometimes white or green, attached by means of a crossbar to a pole which in turn was crowned by an eagle or some other symbol. The vexillum raised on the commander's tent was the signal to march into battle. In the 4th century AD the Roman Empire officially accepted Christianity and also changed its symbols. The vexillum was superseded by the "labarum" which was of similar appearance but which had a larger piece of cloth, richly adorned with gold and silver and bearing the sign of the cross, and sometimes also the inscription "In hoc signo vinces" ("In this sign thou shalt conquer"). The eagle on top of the pole was replaced by the Greek letters XP, the monogram representing Christ's name. A labarum was used for the first time by Emperor Constantine the Great soon after the victory over his adversary Maxentius in AD 312 near Rome. (According to a well-known legend the labarum was actually used during the battle.) In Europe, flags similar to the vexillum and the labarum were in use until the 9th century, although flags of different shapes were very often used simultaneously. Thus in AD 507 the chief campaign sign of the Franks was the blue mantle of St Martin borne on a crossbar; this mantle was taken from the saint's chapel by King Clovis, and its tradition continued in France until the defeat by the English at Poitiers in 1356.

It was from China that Europeans came to know flags of basically the same appearance as those of today, partly through the Huns (Attila, their leader from AD 434, used a white flag bearing a golden eagle) and partly through the Arabs, who first saw flags which came via Persia before the birth of Islam. Since this religion forbids the depiction of living creatures, Arab flags bore various abstract patterns or inscriptions. Mohammed's grandsons used green triangular flags with fringes, sometimes showing the traditional double swords. Green became the colour of the Fatimids while the Abbasids had black flags, the Omayyads white and the Hashimites red.

The continuing Christianization of Europe was marked by the appearance of the so-called "pallium" which was a narrow flag blessed by the Pope. It preceded the battle flag known as a "gonfanon". The flag Montjoie, given to Charlemagne by Pope Leo III in 800, was in fact a gonfanon. Its name is derived from Mons Gaudii (in French, Mont Joie) where this ceremony took place. The name of another kind of flag — the "Oriflamme" (flame of gold) — is derived from its shining golden-red colour. Its tradition was without doubt carried on in the red crosses used at the beginning of the crusades by the French knights.

The frequent use of flags is proved by the famous Bayeux Tapestry, made in 1070-80, picturing the Battle of Hastings in 1066 in which William the Conqueror, Duke of Normandy, defeated the Anglo-Saxons. This tapestry shows a gonfanon, which looks very much like the Raven Flag, and the Dragon Standard in the hands of the Anglo-Saxons.

Even before the crusades Pope Urban II suggested in 1095 that all the participants in the expeditions to the Holy Land should carry the sign of a red cross on their shoulder or breast. These crosses also adorned the small gonfanons used by the crusaders, and later the narrow pennons attached to their lances. The crusades (1096 – 1291) played an important role in the evolution of flags, and the Third Crusade (1189 – 92) especially brought about new features in flags. On 13 January 1188 its leaders had agreed in Gisors in France that all their nations would go into battle under the sign of the cross but that different colours would be used for each of their armies. Philip II Augustus of France kept the red cross on a white field; Henry II of England took a white cross on a red field; and Count Philip of Flanders had a green cross on a white field. Nevertheless, the English went to the Third Crusade under a red cross on a white flag, and the Roman Emperor Henry VI placed a white cross on a red flag when he prepared for the Fourth Crusade. This flag was later used as a general symbol of the Cristian cause, and finally of the Holy Roman Empire. (As early as 1228, however, Emperor Frederick II used a yellow flag with a black eagle). In many countries the red flag with a white cross was held in great esteem and occasionally was used as a symbol of the struggle for freedom, as was the case in Switzerland. In France a white cross on red is known to have been used in 1375; later, white on blue was also used.

In the middle of the 12th century, during the Second Crusade, knights began to adopt personal signs which conformed to certain rules; these signs mostly represented animals and were placed on shields. These "charges", which enabled warriors to be recognized in battle, were also placed on flags. Both the charge and the colour of the flag were always identical with those of the shield, the flag simply echoing the shield. In the 13th century heraldic flags called "banners" came into use: these were square, or rectangular with their length greater than their width. A special type of banner appeared in the 14th century, especially during the Hussite period in Bohemia; these had a horizontal bar which kept them spread even when there was no wind, and their fly was often prolonged and sometimes ended with a tassel.

Pompous feudal banners were replaced at the beginning of the 16th century by banners used by the "Landsknecht" military units. The latter were mostly rectangular, brightly coloured, flying from a short pole, and measuring some 2 metres by 3 metres (6 ft 7 in by 9 ft 10 in). Mounted units, however, used smaller and simpler standards. The most usual one was called a "cornet", and later a "guidon", which was swallow-tailed. These opened the way for the entrance of national flags which developed during the 18th and (chiefly) the 19th century.

The Netherlands was the first country to use a national flag at sea, and other nations soon followed. It was not until later that national flags were flown on land.

When national flags began to be produced in great quantities, one point remained important — the ease and speed with which they could be manufactured. Consequently flags came to consist only of stripes in the colours of the coat of arms. In the case of simple arms all the colours were usually taken to make a flag but in the case of more complicated arms only the chief colours were used. The most honourable stripe (the top horizontal or the first vertical one in the hoist) was given the colour of the charge, and the next was given the colour of the shield — as in the case of the Polish flag. In the case of a flag with three stripes, the last colour to be used was that of some lesser heraldic detail, e.g. the eagle's claws, the grass, etc. In different countries, however, different rules apply, and there are many exceptions. Sometimes there is no connection at all between the colours of the arms and those of the flag.

Later many flags were created before the coat of arms of the country and sometimes, in a reversal of the classical heraldic tradition, the arms followed the pattern of the flag. In other cases, especially in the new

African states, the coat of arms has no link with the flag at all. In such cases the flag becomes an entirely new factor and its colours have a symbolism of their own. This is a new feature. Colours are no longer rigidly bound to a specific symbolism and, for the sake of differentiation, the range of shades used has now gone far beyond the traditional heraldic colours, while the meanings of individual colours vary from flag to flag. Sometimes additional symbolic meaning is even given to colours taken over from coats of arms in the classical way.

In feudal times a flag usually represented a ruler, a nobleman, an overlord or a state; as a rule it had little to do with the people. It was the French Revolution, however, which aroused the national consciousness in this respect and brought about a change. Revolutionary flags then began to be created which became political symbols of the people, and these gave rise to national flags which each individual can consider as his or her own. National flags thus became sacred symbols. Since then many people have sacrificed their lives for their national flag and its honour.

National and state flags are of course the most common types. The difference between them is simple: the national flag can be used, provided certain rules are not violated, by every citizen of the country, while the state flag is destined solely for official use and may be flown exclusively by state institutions and offices. Sometimes state flags differ from national flags by the inclusion of a coat of arms (or one of its components). Very often, however, the same design functions as both national and state flag. In this book, preference is given to the more complicated version, where one exists.

In the text, flags are described in the accepted vexillological way, i.e. from the viewpoint of the observer, from left to right and from top to bottom. They are drawn hoisted on a vertical staff and they fly from left to right. Consequently the obverse side is seen (this is also true for the flags of the Islamic countries). The reverse is described when it differs from the obverse (e.g. Paraguay and the USSR).

The field of a flag is divided into five notional parts: the hoist, the centre, the fly, the top and the bottom. The normal rectangular flag has four edges — the hoist edge, the fly edge, the top edge and the bottom edge — and four corners — the upper and lower hoist and the upper and lower fly. A flag may be divided into horizontal or vertical stripes. Their width is expressed in ratio form, e.g. 1 : 2 : 1, but no ratio is given when they are of equal width.

The basic colours appearing on flags are white, yellow, red, blue, green, orange, brown and purple; different shades are common from country to country. Silver is usually replaced by white, and gold by yellow; this also applies to arms when they are parts of flags. Occasionally silver can be represented by grey (the silver George Cross on the flag of Malta), and gold by deep yellow (GDR). In black-and-white drawings the usual heraldic hatching is used.

Red is the most common colour in the flags of independent countries (appearing in about 80 per cent of them), followed by white (70 per cent) and blue (45 per cent). About one-half of all flags consist of three colours; 27 per cent are bicoloured; and only one consists of a single colour. No flag has more than six colours, if the traditional heraldic colours of a coat of arms are ignored. About one-half of the flags have a design not older than twenty-five years, and about 20 per cent date from the previous twenty-five years. Only some 10 per cent of the designs are older than one hundred years, and only a very few are older than two hundred years.

The most common proportions are 2 : 3 (this applies to more than half of all flags), about 20 per cent of flags having dimensions of 1 : 2 and only 9 per cent 3 : 5. Two flags alone are square, and one is neither rectangular not square. About 10 per cent of flags bear a full armorial achievement.

Certain groups of countries adopted the same colours, the only difference being their arrangement and order. The so-called pan-African colours first adopted by Ethiopia at the end of the past century were taken over in 1957 by Ghana and later by a number of other countries. The pan-Arab colours were used for the first time in 1918 by Hejaz, and are used today by a number of Arab states, while the Egyptian variant of the colours of Arab liberation was accepted by other countries too. The green colour of Islam dominates the flags of Libya, Saudi Arabia, Pakistan, Mauretania and the Comoros but can also be seen on many other flags. The Russian colours (white, blue and red) introduced by Peter the Great were taken over by many Slavonic nations. The colours of the United Provinces of Central America (1823—39) became those of all the successor states, while the colours of Great Colombia, originally introduced in Venezuela in 1806 by Francisco de Miranda, are still seen on the flags of the countries created when that union came to an end.

The study of flags goes a long way back in time, but its name, vexillology, was coined in 1959 by Dr Whitney Smith in the USA The first book about flags is the manuscript, dating from about 1350, of an anonymous Spanish Franciscan monk, entitled "Libro de conoscimiento de todos los reynos e tierras e señorias que son por el mundo e de señales e armas". It contains pictures of 110 flags of various towns and countries. Later flags appeared in "portolanos" and atlases, and at the end of the 17th century the first flag charts were printed, in which flags were hand-coloured. Siebmacher's "Grosses und allgemeines Wappenbuch"(1854—1961) also contains, apart from thousands of arms, numerous flags. Nevertheless heraldry treated flags only as a subsidiary branch and this caused the vexillologists to separate from the mother science until they achieved complete independence in 1962 when the Flag Research Center, with its periodical "The Flag Bulletin", was founded. Vexillology now has its own terminology, and there are vexillological societies in many countries; in the United Kingdom it is The Flag Institute at Chester. The central vexillological institution is the International Federation of Vexillological Associations (FIAV), which now organizes regular international congresses. Vexillology is more than an auxiliary historical science because it also embraces aspects of international and constitutional law. Heraldry, however, will always play an important role in vexillology because both are closely connected.

Many countries have developed their own flag code which requires that their national and state flags should always be treated with the utmost reverence and honour. Strangely enough this is not the case in the United Kingdom where only ships of the Royal Navy are required to comply with a strict flag etiquette, which among other things prescribes that ensigns should be hoisted at 8 a.m. and lowered at sunset. A ship also salutes another ship in a prescribed way, i.e. by dipping its flag. A special code applies to military colours.

Care should be taken when more than one national flag is hoisted: they should all be of equal size and on equally high staffs. In no circumstances should two national flags be hoisted on a single staff, one underneath the other, and no national flag should ever be dishonoured in any way, or hoisted in improper places.

Coats of arms

The history of coats of arms is also very old, but arms as we know them today are not an inheritance from Ancient Greece or Rome. They developed during the Second Crusade in the middle of the 12th century when the crusaders encountered old Oriental traditions. Originally arms were purely personal or family signs, reserved only for nobility. Among the first owners of a coat of arms was usually (but not necessarily) the sovereign. The main component of a coat of arms was the shield, a part of the knight's armament. Subsequently other components were added — a helmet with a crest, mantling, supporters, scrolls with mottoes, etc. The use of the shield with an heraldic charge, as a part of armament, has diminished since the 15th century and the coat of arms has increasingly assumed the role of symbolizing its owner.

From about the 14th century onwards, sovereigns' coats of arms came to symbolize their country, and consequently they later became symbols of the country's inhabitants. The arms remained as such symbols even when the reigning dynasty changed, new rulers taking over the arms of their predecessors. Thus state coats of arms have developed. In some European countries the sovereign's arms are identical with the state coat of arms. In addition there are often the greater, the lesser and, sometimes, the medium arms. The greater arms include the supporters and the motto, and may be placed on a pavilion; the medium arms have no pavilion; and the lesser arms have no supporters. Arms have often

15

remained symbols of sovereignty in spite of changing times and social conditions. Many European countries still go on using arms dating from feudal times although their inhabitants have long since abandoned a feudal way of life. A coat of arms bears witness to historical traditions and national pride which have survived for centuries. Other countries, however, abandoned their old arms with a change of political system and they created new symbols, sometimes with no regard for heraldic customs. France is an example of this: since the middle of the 19th century the symbol of state sovereignty has been encircled by the Order of the Legion of Honour. The Soviet Union also has an altogether different coat of arms from that of Tsarist Russia, the change of the social order being documented not only symbolically but also by the inscription. The Soviet arms have served as the model for both the general design and the components of the arms of a number of socialist countries. Not even the arms of Italy comply with heraldic requirements, although the white five-pointed star is a reminder of the heraldic traditions of the House of Savoy.

The American countries liberated themselves from their European colonial domination at a time when European heraldry was on the decline. This may be the reason why their arms — chiefly those of South American countries — are so very unheraldic; they are often oval in shape, containing a number of flags, and even realistically portrayed landscapes. Heraldry should use heraldic charges, not pictures of buildings or scenery. The countries of Asia, for a long time isolated from Europe, also differ in their arms from the concepts of European heraldry, and are often influenced by local traditions. New Arab states, however, have tried to imitate the recent Egyptian pattern. In Africa there is a great variety: on the one hand one finds arms which are European in character, on the other, arms which are no more than the circular state seal. This latter practice is predominant in the former French colonies (Madagascar, Mali, etc.). Arms of the European type are found in some former British colonies (Kenya, Uganda, Tanzania, Botswana and Lesotho), but with indigenous shields.

In countries where heraldic traditions are fully respected, there is usually no single official version of the drawing of the coat of arms, and different stylistic variants are used. On the other hand, in countries with loose heraldic traditions the coat of arms has to adhere to the officially approved form. Strictly speaking, such symbols should not be called coats of arms but rather state badges of sovereignty, especially in cases where the shield, the chief component of a coat of arms, is missing. Still, for practical purposes, these symbols are described as state arms.

EUROPE

ALBANIA (5:7)

ANDORRA (2:3)

AUSTRIA (2:3)

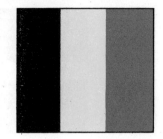

BELGIUM (13:15)

BULGARIA (3:5)

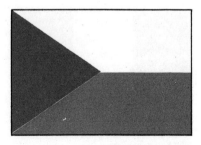

CZECHOSLOVAKIA (2:3)

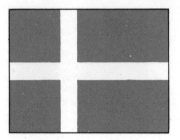

DENMARK (28:37)

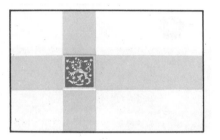

FINLAND (11:18)

FRANCE (2:3)

22

GERMAN DEMOCRATIC REPUBLIC(3:5)

GERMANY, FEDERAL REPUBLIC OF(3:5)

GREECE (2:3)

HUNGARY (2:3)

ICELAND (18:25)

IRELAND (1:2)

ITALY (2:3)

LIECHTENSTEIN (3:5)

LUXEMBOURG(3:5)

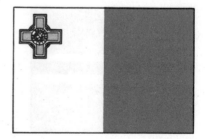

MALTA(2:3)

MONACO (4:5)

NETHERLANDS (2:3)

NORWAY (8:11)

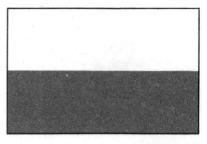

POLAND (5:8)

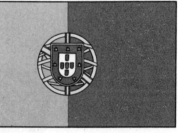

PORTUGAL (2:3)

ROMANIA (2:3)

29

SAN MARINO (3:4)

SOVIET UNION (1:2)

SPAIN (2:3)

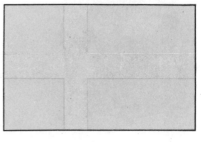

SWEDEN (5:8)

SWITZERLAND (1:1)

UNITED KINGDOM(1:2)

VATICAN(1:1)

WEST BERLIN (3:5)

YUGOSLAVIA (1:2)

Åland Islands(17:26)

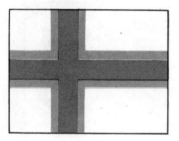

Faeroe Islands(8:11)

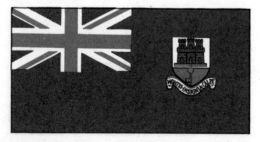

Gibraltar (1:2)

Guernsey (1:2)

Isle of Man (1:2)

Jersey (1:2)

ALBANIA
Socialist republic

The Albanian flag is red featuring a black double-headed eagle, surmounted by a red five-pointed star edged with yellow. The eagle is taken from the state coat of arms and was originally the symbol of the Byzantine Empire. From 1463 Skanderbeg, who became the Albanian national hero for successfully fighting back repeated Turkish invasions, used the double-headed eagle as his emblem. To this day the Albanians call their country "Shqipëria",which means "land of the eagle", and they proudly call themselves "Shqipëtarë",meaning "descendants of the eagle". Red symbolizes the blood the Albanians shed during their struggles against the Turks and, later, other occupying forces, and the five-pointed star stands for the ideas of communism. Skanderbeg's flag was revived when the country obtained independence in 1912 and the flag in its present form has been used since 1946.

ANDORRA
Principality with the joint heads of state being the President of the French Republic and the Bishop of Urgel in Spain

The state flag has three vertical stripes of blue, yellow and red, and in the centre there is the Andorran coat of arms with a coronet. The shield has four quarters the first is white with a gold mitre and crozier representing the Bishop of Urgel; the second is yellow with three vertical red stripes from the arms of the counts of Foix; the third is yellow with four vertical red stripes from the arms of Catalonia (the Andorrans are Catalans); and in the fourth, also yellow, quarter there are two red cows from the arms of the counts of Béarn. From 1278 Andorra stood under the joint protection of the Bishop of Urgel and the French counts of Foix (who in 1290 were superseded by the counts of Béarn, then by the French crown, and now by the French president). The symbolism of this joint administration is reflected in the colours of the flag: blue and red are taken from the French flag, yellow and red from the flag of Spain. The first Andorran flag of 1806 consisted of two horizontal stripes, yellow and red (colours of Foix), to which a blue stripe was added in 1866 (Napoleon III is reputed to have suggested this), and at the same time the stripes were made perpendicular. Occasionally a flag with horizontal stripes appears even now, featuring the coronet of the

Foix family in the centre; this version of the Andorran flag is taken to be the Spanish one. A more recent explanation of the colours is that blue stands for the French flag, red for the Spanish, and yellow for the flag of the Vatican since the religion of the majority of Andorrans is Roman Catholicism.

AUSTRIA
Federal republic

The Austrian flag, one of the oldest in the world, consists of three horizontal stripes of red, white and red. Its pattern and colours correspond to those of the historical shield in the state coat of arms. According to a legend which prevailed in the late Middle Ages, Duke Leopold V of Babenberg fought so bravely against the Saracens at Acre in the Holy Land during the crusade of 1191 that his entire surcoat was stained with blood except for the part beneath his belt, which remained white. It was from this bloodstained coat that the Austrian colours were taken. In 1786 the red-white-red flag became the Austrian state flag and ensign and, until 1869, the merchant flag (which had as an additional charge the shield with a crown); in Austria-Hungary it served as the national flag, the state flag being black and yellow. Since 1918 it has been the Austrian national flag; if the state coat of arms is borne on the white stripe it becomes the state flag. The present coat of arms of Austria is a black eagle with a red tongue, gold claws, wearing a gold civic crown and holding in its claws a gold sickle and a gold hammer as symbols of the peasants and workers; the crown represents the middle class. Since 1945 the eagle has had broken silver chains on its legs to commemorate the liberation from Nazism. It is charged on the breast with the red shield with a silver central stripe which appeared during the reign of the last Babenbergs, Leopold VI (reigned 1198−1230) and Frederick II (reigned 1230−46); from that time the eagle has remained the coat of arms of the dukes of Austria and was taken over by the Habsburgs.

BELGIUM
Kingdom

The Belgian tricolour has three vertical stripes of black, yellow and red. Its colours are taken from the arms of Brabant, Flanders and Hainaut, and they appeared for the first time − as horizontal stripes − during the Brabant uprising against Austria in 1789. The present arrangement has been known since 1830 (in 1831 it was made legal by the constitution) and undoubtedly reflects that of the French tricolour.

BULGARIA
People's republic

The flag of Bulgaria consists of three horizontal stripes of white, green and red with the Bulgarian state coat of arms as modified in 1971 in the hoist of the white stripe. The arms comprise a wreath of wheat ears enclosing an oval in the blue field of which there is a gold lion rampant, with red tongue and claws, above part of a white cogwheel. The lion is an old Bulgarian symbol and stands for power, courage and heroism. It has been the official symbol of Bulgaria since 1879. The cogwheel and wheat ears symbolize the union of the workers and the peasants, the former symbol emphasizing the industrial character of the country today. The red scroll and the tricolour in the national colours, which binds the stalks of the wheat, recall the struggle for liberation from the fascist monarchy and the building of socialism. The two dates on the red scroll refer to the foundation of the first Bulgarian state by Tsar Asparuch (681), and the liberation of the country and the victory of the socialist revolution (1944). Blue stands for the people's fight for peace, and the five-pointed red star at the top symbolizes the ideas of communism and the solidarity of the Bulgarian people with all the workers of the world. The three--coloured Bulgarian flag (without the coat of arms) was created after the so-called Braila tricolour of 1877 and has been in use since 1878. It resembles — as do a number of other flags of the southern Slavs — the old Russian tricolour; indeed, Bulgaria owes her liberation in 1878 from Turkish rule to the Russian armies. The blue stripe of the Russian flag was replaced by a green one, i.e. by the colour of freedom. Green also symbolizes fertility, agriculture and the forests of Bulgaria. Red is the colour of the blood shed for liberation; it is also a symbol of the victorious revolution and of readiness to defend the successes of socialism. White signifies love of work, peace and freedom. The coat of arms has appeared on the flag since 1948.

CZECHOSLOVAKIA
Socialist federal republic

The Czechoslovak flag consists of two horizontal stripes, white over red, with a blue triangle in the hoist, the apex of which is in the centre of the flag. The colours and exact shape of the flag were established by law on 29 February 1920 and the flag was officially adopted on 30 March 1920. It was confirmed without change on 17 November 1960.

The free Czechoslovak state, created on 28 October 1918, was initially represented by the old white-over-red flag of Bohemia. The following year a commission was set up to determine the design of the national flag. Legalization of the Bohemian flag was rejected because white and red stripes were already used in the flags of neighbouring Poland and

Austria. The commission decided to add blue since these three traditionally Slavonic colours were used in Slovakia and blue also featured in the arms of Moravia. The shape chosen for blue was a triangle, which was one of the oldest charges in Bohemian heraldry and also symbolised the three peaks depicted in the arms of Slovakia. The triangle originally extended to one-third of the flag's length but in January 1920 it was increased to one-half of the length, the proportions 2 : 3 being maintained. According to one contemporary interpretation of the colours, white stands for purity, red symbolizes the blood shed for the freedom of the country and blue represents the clear sky.

DENMARK
Kingdom

The Danish flag is red with a white Scandinavian cross; it is commonly called the Dannebrog which originally meant something like "red cloth" or "red flag". It recalls the time of the crusades, when it first appeared, and it is considered to be the oldest permanently used flag in the world. Its probable origin is in the war flag of the Holy Roman Empire which looked upon Denmark as its vassal. According to a legend, which did not arise until the 16th century, the flag fell from heaven into the hands of the Danish archbishop Anders Sunesen on 15 June 1219 in a battle which Valdemar II, King of Denmark, fought during a crusade against the Estonians at Lyndanisse (on the site of present-day Tallin). It happened just as the Danish armies were weakening and it is said that the miraculously sent flag gave them enough strength to win the battle. According to another version, on the eve of the battle King Valdemar saw a white cross appearing on flaming red skies as a good omen for the coming encounter, and the next day the Danish armies actually went to victory under such a flag. For this reason 15 June is still celebrated as Dannebrog Day. The oldest documents showing this flag, however, date from the middle of the 14th century when the flags of Austria and of England were already in existence. The state flag and ensign are swallow-tailed. The Danish flag is also used in Greenland.

FINLAND
Republic

The present flag of Finland was introduced in 1918, following an earlier version of 1861. (The old Finnish flag depicted a gold lion on a red field, taken from the state arms.) According to the words of the poet Zacharias Topelius, white symbolizes the Finnish winter and the endless snow-covered plains, and the blue reflects both the country's relations with the other Nordic countries, which also have the Scandinavian cross on their flags, and the colour of the lakes and rivers of Finland. The currently used national flag is without the coat of arms, but this appears in square form at the intersection of the blue cross in the state flag and ensign. These arms are connected with the historical coat of arms of the Grand Duchy of Finland, which date back to 1557. On a red shield there is a crowned gold lion rampant holding a silver sword in its right paw which is clad in armour. Beneath the lion there is a scimitar, which, as an oriental weapon, represented the danger threatening the country from the Tartars, Swedes and other enemies. The nine white roses stand for the nine historical regions of Finland. In 1978 the light blue colour of the flag was changed to a darker blue, and the shield of the arms was made into a square field edged with yellow.

FRANCE
Republic

The French flag, the well-known tricolour with vertical stripes coloured blue, white and red, has its origins in the revolutionary year 1789 when, in the City Hall of Paris, King Louis XVI added the Parisian blue-and-red cockade to the white one of the Bourbons which he wore and this new combination of colours was welcomed by the people (in those times cockades were seen more often than flags). In the flags that were used over the next few years both the order and the position of the stripes varied. Following the proclamation of the Republic, however, the painter J.-L. David, authorized by the Convention, gave the tricolour its present arrangement which was first seen in 1794. The royal white flag came back into use during the Restoration (1814 – 15) and again, after Napoleon's hundred days' rule and final downfall at Waterloo in 1815, until the July Revolution of 1830 when the tricolour was hoisted once more. As late as in 1848, however, the order of the stripes was blue, red and white for a short period. Originally the perpendicular stripes were of equal width but, seen from a distance, they appeared to be unequal owing to the differing intensity of the colours. The flag used at sea was, therefore, optically balanced in 1853 so that the blue stripe was given 30 per cent, and the red one 37 per cent of the area of the flag (their widths were in the proportions 90 : 99 : 111). These proportions are still used in the naval ensign while the stripes of the national flag have been of equal width since 1946. The colours or the pattern of the French flag have been the direct or indirect inspiration of quite a number of other flags, not only in the past (Haiti, the Dominican Republic, Norway, Paraguay, Costa Rica and Thailand) but also quite recently (some of the former French colonies in Africa).

The French flag is also used as the only official flag in the Overseas Departments of France — Mayotte (which has special status), Réunion, Guadeloupe, Martinique, French Guiana, and St Pierre and Miquelon —

and her Overseas Territories — French Polynesia, New Caledonia, Wallis and Futuna, and the Southern and Antarctic Territories.

GERMAN DEMOCRATIC REPUBLIC
People's republic

Since 1949 the state flag of the German Democratic Republic has been a tricolour with horizontal stripes of black, red and deep yellow (officially gold) to which the state coat of arms of the GDR was added in 1959. The arms comprise a gold hammer (symbol of the workers) and a pair of dividers (symbol of the intelligentsia) placed in a red circle, and surrounded by a wreath of wheat ears (representing the peasants) which is entwined with a tricolour of the German colours. These are now given the following interpretation: black symbolizes the past of the German nation; red stands for today's struggle for the nation's happy future; and gold signifies the age of communism. The colours were taken from the uniforms of Lützow's student volunteers in the war with Napoleon (1813 – 1815), who used black-coloured civilian clothes with red epaulettes and piping, and brass buttons. These units did not have their own flags but they founded the tradition of the tricolour which then appeared in 1832. In the revolutionary year 1848 the colours were given one of their interpretations in these lines in a poem by F. Freiligrath: "The powder is black, the blood is red, the flame has a golden glow". It is true that Bismarck replaced this flag in 1867 with a black-white-red tricolour but it was reintroduced in 1919 by the Weimar Republic, which used it until 1933. After the creation of the GDR these revolutionary colours were established by the constitution of 1949.

GERMANY, FEDERAL REPUBLIC OF
Federal republic

The flag of the Federal Republic of Germany was introduced in 1949 and, as with the flag of the GDR, it follows the colours of the Weimar Republic used from 1919 until 1933. It is a tricolour consisting of horizontal stripes coloured black, red and gold. When the state arms of the Federal Republic are borne on the flag it becomes the state flag and ensign (the latter, in addition, being swallow-tailed).

GREECE
Republic

The Greek flag consists of nine horizontal stripes — five blue alternating with four white ones — with a white cross in a blue square canton. At the beginning of the rising against Turkey in 1821 a blue flag with a white cross was hoisted as a symbol of opposition to the Ottoman crescent. However, the cross was soon put in a canton on a striped flag which was officially adopted in March 1822. It is meant to symbolize "God's wisdom, freedom and the country". The nine stripes are apparently a reminder of the Greek revolutionary slogan ELEUTHERÍA E THÁNATOS ("Liberty or death") which has nine syllables. (According to other interpretations the stripes represent the nine stripes on Achilles' shield, the nine muses or the nine years of the war for the freedom of the country, 1821 – 30.) Blue is the symbol of the sea and of the cloudless southern sky which gave the Greek patriots the idea of an uprising; white denotes the purity of their aims in the struggle for freedom and independence; and the cross in the canton points to faith and the religiousness of the Greeks. The shade of blue has often changed, however; on the accession of the Bavarian Prince Otto I of the House of Wittelsbach to the Greek throne in 1833, light blue, which together with white are the colours of Bavaria, was decreed. The white cross on a blue field was used as the Greek national flag on land until 1970, while the flag with the stripes was hoisted at sea, in Greek ports and abroad. From 1970 until 1975 the striped version became the only Greek flag and a dark shade of blue was used. Between 1975 and 1978 the blue flag with the cross was restored for all purposes; in practice, however, the striped flag was also sometimes used. The law of 1978 finally returned to the striped flag, stating that it is universally valid, but an intermediate shade of blue is now used.

HUNGARY
People's republic

The Hungarian flag with its horizontal stripes of red, white and green is identical with the old flag of Hungary, the colours of which date from the reign of King Matthias II at the beginning of the 17th century. The flag embodies the colours of the old Hungarian coat of arms, which are the colours of freedom. Since 1848 this tricolour has been used as the national flag. In conformity with the present coat of arms the colours have been given a new meaning — from the top down — readiness for sacrifice (red) and the pure character of the nation (white) are like sun and rain to the promisingly green vegetation which, after ripening in peace, will bring the rich fruits of communism. Since 1957 there have been no arms on the Hungarian flag.

ICELAND
Republic

The flag is blue with a red Scandinavian cross edged with white. Blue is a traditional colour of Iceland, representing the sea and the summits of the mountains reaching up into the sky; red symbolizes the still active volcanoes and their red-hot lava; and white stands for the geysers and icebergs. The cross stresses Iceland's links with the other Nordic countries, and the red colour of the cross recalls the flag of Norway from which country the island was colonized and to which it belonged until the 13th century when both countries came under Danish domination. This is why the pattern of the flag of Iceland is identical with that of Norway, except that the colours are reversed. The flag was created in 1913 and was officially adopted in 1915.

IRELAND
Republic

The Irish tricolour has vertical stripes of green, white and orange. Green symbolizes the Emerald Isle and the Catholic majority of its population; orange, taken from the colour of the House of Orange-Nassau, represents the Protestants, while the white stripe in the centre signifies the need for peace and understanding between the two religious groups; for this reason this flag is expressly described as unionist. According to some proposals the white colour was to stand for the minority of Irish Presbyterians. The colours appeared for the first time in 1830 (previously a green flag with a yellow harp was more common) and came to be more widely used as a flag from 1848 when it was flown together with the French tricolour to celebrate the February revolution in Paris that year (a leader of Young Ireland, T.F. Meagher, brought the tricolour straight from revolutionary Paris). The Irish tricolour became the symbol of free Ireland after the Easter week rising in 1916. In 1920 the present arrangement of the colours was established, and in 1922 this tricolour became the national flag of the dominion called the Irish Free State. This flag was officially confirmed in the Constitution of 1937 and it remained unchanged when the Republic of Ireland was established in 1949.

ITALY
Republic

The Italian tricolour consists of vertical stripes of green, white and red. It was modelled on the French flag but green was used instead of blue (since the French Revolution the former colour had come to be regarded as the symbol of freedom, equality and the new political order). This change of colour took place in 1796 when the Lombard National Guard and later the Italian voluntary Lombard Legion were formed; it is said that the colours were suggested by Napoleon whose favourite colour was green (a similar tricolour had already appeared during the students' demonstrations in Bologna as early as 1795). In 1797 the green-white-red colours became the flag of the Cisalpine Republic, then in 1802 of the Italian Republic which became the Kingdom of Italy in 1805, lasting until 1814. The tricolour flag was restored in 1848 when Victor Emmanuel II, King of Sardinia-Piedmont, adopted it as his flag, placing in its centre the coat of arms of his House of Savoy — a silver cross on a red shield — with a blue border. In this form the tricolour became the flag of united Italy in 1861; only in 1946 when the country became a republic was the royal coat of arms removed from the flag.

LIECHTENSTEIN
Principality

Since 1937 the flag of Liechtenstein has consisted of two horizontal stripes, blue over red, with a yellow princely crown in the upper hoist. The crown was originally added in order to prevent confusion with the then flag of Haiti (during the Olympic Games in Berlin in 1936). Blue and red are Liechtenstein's national colours and were confirmed in the constitution of 1921. Blue symbolizes the sky; red stands for the glow of the evening fires; and the crown represents the union of the people, the state and the reigning dynasty. Although the flag is often hung in the style of a gonfalon, i.e. displayed vertically from a horizontal cross-bar, the crown always remains upright. In 1982 a new flag for official use by the government and parliament was created. This has two horizontal stripes, blue over red, and displays the full armorial achievement of the principality.

LUXEMBOURG
Grand Duchy

The flag consists of three horizontal stripes of red, white and light blue, the colours being taken from the state coat of arms. Until 1890 the flag was absolutely identical with that of the Netherlands, with which country Luxembourg was united between 1815 and 1890, but from then on a much lighter shade of blue was introduced in order to differentiate between the two flags. The flag of Luxembourg was inspired by the French flag; at first a different order of colours was used but the present order has prevailed since 1845.

MALTA
Republic within the British Commonwealth

The flag consists of two vertical stripes of white and red with a grey (representing silver) George Cross edged with red in the upper hoist.

The medallion in the centre of the cross features St George on horseback sorrounded by the words FOR GALLANTRY. This decoration was awarded to the islands by King George VI on 15 April 1942 for the bravery of the Maltese during the concentrated German and Italian air raids in the first years of World War II. The flag in this form was introduced in 1964 when Malta gained her independence. From 1943 to 1964 the cross was placed on a blue square canton, and when this canton was deleted the cross was separated from the white field by the red border. The colours of the flag correspond to the shield of the former coat of arms but they have been attributed to the Norman Count Roger of Sicily (cousin of William the Conqueror) who landed on the island in 1090, liberating it from the Muslims.

Malta

MONACO
Principality

The flag of Monaco has two horizontal stripes, red over white. The colours are taken from the arms of the princely House of Grimaldi and have been established since 1339. The flag was probably created in 1815 and was finally approved in 1881. Today it is identical, apart from its proportions, with the flag of Indonesia, and Monaco protested against the introduction of the Indonesian flag when it appeared in 1945.

NETHERLANDS
Kingdom

The Dutch flag consists of three horizontal stripes coloured red, white and blue. It originates from the time of the revolt of the Dutch Protestant provinces, under the leadership of Prince William of Orange, against Spanish rule. The prince's flag — sometimes only orange but usually a tricolour of orange, white and blue — was first referred to in 1572.

After the liberation of the seven northern provinces from Spanish overlordship and the creation of the Republic of the United Netherlands (1581), the so-called "Prinsvlag"("prince's flag") in the livery colours of the House of Orange was used as a symbol of the states-general side by side with a flag bearing the arms of the Free Netherlands. In 1597 the Prinsvlag was established as the only Dutch flag. About 1630, and especially after 1648 when Spain recognized the independence of the Netherlands, the orange stripe was often replaced by a red one for the sake of better visibility (although political factors may have constituted the main reason for the change). In 1796 the use of the orange colour was specifically forbidden. The original colours of the Dutch flag have been preserved to this day in the flag of South Africa as a reminder of Dutch colonization. In 1937 the dark blue of the Dutch flag was replaced by cobalt blue.

The Dutch flag, being the first republican tricolour in the world and a symbol of freedom, served as the model for all other tricolours, including the French one, and the pre-1917 Russian flag was based on it too. When Peter the Great, Tsar of Russia, returned home after his stay in the Netherlands, he made use of what he had learned to build his own fleet, and he even suggested that the Russian merchant flag should be based on the Dutch flag, merely altering the order of the stripes to make it a white-blue-red tricolour. Later on, this also became the Russian state and national flag. In the pan-Slavonic era of the past century, those Slavonic nations which were not independent took this tricolour as the inspiration for their own flags, some being exactly the same, others having the stripes in a different order. The first of these nations was that of the Serbs in 1835, followed by those of the Montenegrins, Croats, Slovenes, Slovaks and Bulgarians (the last-mentioned replacing the blue stripe with a green one). Thus the Dutch flag even had an indirect influence on the flags of some Slavonic nations.

NORWAY
Kingdom

The Norwegian flag is red with a blue Scandinavian cross edged with white. It resembles the Danish flag because Norway was under Danish rule until 1814 when it was acquired by Sweden, with which country it remained united until 1905. Nevertheless, the colours of the Norwegian flag are also the colours of the French revolutionary tricolour, and are therefore considered to be the colours of freedom. In its present form the flag was accepted by the Norwegian parliament in 1821 as the merchant flag, but its use was limited to the coastal waters; on the high seas Norwegian ships had to fly the flag of the Norwegian — Swedish union which was the flag of Sweden with the symbol of the union in the canton. Between 1844 and 1898 both the Norwegian and Swedish flags had a revised symbol of this union in the canton. In 1898 it finally became possible for Norway to readopt the flag of 1821 as a purely Norwegian flag and also to use it as the national flag. The Norwegian flag served as the model for the flag of Iceland but the latter's colours are reversed. The Norwegian flag alone is flown on the islands of Svalbard (the Spitsbergen archipelago) and Jan Mayen, both of which form part of the kingdom, and in the dependencies, namely, Queen Maud Land, Bouvet Island and Peter I Island.

POLAND
People's republic

The national flag of Poland consists of two horizontal stripes, white over red, the colours being taken from the state coat of arms. They became the Polish national colours in 1831 but a flag composed of them was not introduced until 1919. It has sometimes been interpreted as an allegory of the white eagle rising above the setting sun, at other times as a union of the highest values of the human spirit, and as the sacred sacrifice of human blood for freedom. Today it is explained as an expression of the Polish people's wish to live in peace and socialism.

PORTUGAL
Republic

The Portuguese flag, dating from 1910, has two vertical stripes, green in the hoist (two-fifths of the length), and red in the fly (three-fifths of the length). The shield and armillary sphere (a medieval nautical instrument) from the state coat of arms are placed on the dividing line. The original arms of Portugal, the "quina", had a silver shiels charged with five blue escutcheons, each charged in turn with five silver discs. The escutcheons are arranged in a cross, and this recalls the country's re-christianization following the victory of the first king of Portugal, Afonso I, over five Moorish princes at Ourique in 1139. Originally the silver discs were probably nothing more than decoration but several explanations provide differing symbolic meanings, such as the five wounds of Christ, and victory over five enemies. In 1258, following the marriage of Afonso III with Princess Beatriz of Castile, the shield was given the red border with seven golden Castilian castles. The shield and border were placed on a golden armillary sphere; this was a pictorial device of King Manuel I (1495 — 1521) and commemorates Prince Henry the Navigator who instigated the voyages of discovery that led to the founding of the former Portuguese empire overseas. The red colour of the flag symbolizes the revolution of 1910 which gave birth to the republic, and green is a symbol of hope. Both colours are taken from the standard which was hoisted on the battleship "Adamastor" at the beginning of the Portuguese revolution in 1910. The Portuguese flag is the only one flown in Macao.

ROMANIA
Socialist republic

The Romanian flag consists of three vertical stripes of dark blue, yellow and red with the state coat of arms in the centre. The national colours date from 1834, being the colours of Moldavia (blue and red) and of Wallachia (blue and yellow). In 1848 they were combined into a blue-yellow-red tricolour arranged horizontally. Sometimes this flag is interpreted simply as an adoption of the colours featuring in the arms of the princes of Wallachia. The flag was officially accepted in 1859 when Wallachia and Moldavia were united into a single principality which took the name Romania in 1861. It was not until 1866 that the stripes were arranged vertically, following the French tricolour. When the Congress of Berlin in 1878 confirmed the independence of Romania, its existing flag was recognized. The colours of the flag were interpreted in this way: blue was the symbol of the clear sky, yellow stood for the mineral wealth of the country and red for the gallantry of its people. A coat of arms has always been placed in the flag's centre. The present one dates from 1948 and shows, within a wreath of wheat ears, a rural scene with an oil derrick, a forest and mountain peaks, all in their true colours, with the sun rising in the background. Since 1952 these arms have been surmounted by a red five-pointed star. The wreath is entwined with a ribbon in the Romanian national colours, bearing the full name of the state, which is REPUBLICA SOCIALISTA ROMANIA and dates from 1965. The arms are symbolical of the country's natural wealth, and the red star and the name of the state reflect the country's socialist status.

SAN MARINO
Republic

The flag of San Marino dates from about 1797 and its colours — white and blue in two horizontal stripes — are taken from the colours of the coat of arms which is in the middle of the state flag. In the oval shield of the arms there are three green peaks topped by three silver towers representing the towers on the three peaks of Monte Titano — Guaita, Cesta and Montale; each tower is adorned with a white ostrich feather. The blue colour stands for the sky, white for the clouds and the winter snow on Monte Titano. Although San Marino is a republic, a crown forms part of the arms as a symbol of sovereignty. Flanking the shield are sprigs of laurel and oak and beneath it there is a white scroll with the word LIBERTAS ("Liberty") in yellow. This was the usual motto of the Italian city republics. The civil flag does not carry the state arms.

SOVIET UNION
Federation of socialist republics

The Soviet flag is red with a crossed hammer and sickle in yellow surmounted by a red star edged with yellow in the upper hoist (these emblems are taken from the state coat of arms). The hammer and sickle are drawn within an imaginary square with sides equal to one-quarter of the flags width; the tip of the sickle touches the upper side of the square while the handles of both tools end in its bottom corners. The length of the hammer with its handle is three-quarters that of the diagonal of the square. The five-pointed star is drawn within an imaginary circle with a diameter equal to one-eighth of the width of the flag, and which touches the centre of the upper side of the imaginary square. The distance of the vertical axis of the star, and of the intersection of the diagonals of the imaginary square, from the hoist is one-third of the flag's width. Red symbolizes the proletarian revolution, and the hammer and sickle stand for the union of the workers and peasants in an independent state under the leadership of the Communist Party. The five-pointed star is a sign of the unity and international solidarity of the working class in all five continents. The flag was approved in 1923 and finally settled in 1924; the shape of the hammer and sickle was slightly corrected and exactly prescribed in 1955. In 1980 it was stipulated that the hammer, the sickle and the star appear only on the obverse side of the flag, the reverse being all red.

Soviet Union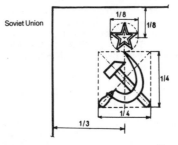

SPAIN
Kingdom

The Spanish flag consists of three horizontal stripes, coloured red, yellow and red in the proportions 1 : 2 : 1, and was derived from the medieval arms of Aragon. According to a legend, after a fight with the Moors the West Frankish King Charles II the Bald (ruled 843 – 77) dipped his fingers in the blood of his wounded ally Count Wilfred I of Aragon and drew them down his plain-coloured shield; thus his coat of arms was created. The red-yellow-red ensign for the navy was introduced in 1785 (with the arms of Castile and Leon), being adopted as the state flag in 1793. The revolution of 1868 substituted purple for the bottom red stripe but after the fall of the republic the royal flag was again used from 1875. The second republic returned to the tricolour composed of three equal stripes of red, yellow and purple but in 1936 General Franco restored the red-yellow-red stripes in the proportions 1 : 2 : 1, to which the coat of arms of Franco's regime was added between 1939 and 1981. The new coat of arms of 1981 has a quartered shield in which the quarters stand for Castile (in red, a gold castle), Leon (in silver, a red lion rampant, crowned gold), Aragon (in gold, four vertical red stripes) and Navarre (in red, gold chains). In the base of the shield is a silver field with a pomegranate representing Granada. A blue inescutcheon with a red border charged with three gold fleurs-de-lis (2 : 1) represents the reigning House of Bourbon. The shield is surmounted by the royal crown which is repeated on the sinister column flanking the shield, while the dexter column is surmounted by the imperial crown. These columns are the so-called Pillars of Hercules, representing Gibraltar and Ceuta, and they are entwined with red scrolls with the motto PLUS ULTRA. In the Middle Ages this read NON PLUS ULTRA ("There is nothing more beyond") since no land was expected beyond Gibraltar. After the discovery of America Emperor Charles V amended this to PLUS ULTRA ("There is more beyond"). On the state flag and ensign the arms are placed slightly towards the hoist (their vertical axis is at a distance equalling one-half of the flag's width from the hoist). The seventeen autonomous regions of Spain now fly their own flags beside the state flag, and in Spanish North Africa the cities of Ceuta and Melilla fly their own city flags beside the state flag.

SWEDEN
Kingdom

The Swedish flag is blue with a yellow Scandinavian cross. It was evidently inspired by the oldest Nordic flag with a cross — the Danish flag — and follows the greater state arms of Sweden in which a gold cross divides the four blue quarters of the shield. It was probably created in 1521, according to tradition, during the struggle with the Danes led by the regent, and later king, Gustavus I Vasa, in whose reign it became very popular. The anniversary of Vasa's coronation on 6 June 1523 is therefore celebrated each year as Swedish Flag Day. Indeed the cross had already appeared on the standards used during the reigns of both Gustavus I Vasa and Erik XIV, and John III decreed that this "golden or yellow cross", which is a traditional part of the coat of arms, should be used in perpetuity on all flags, ensigns and standards. During the reign of Gustavus II Adolphus this flag began to be generally used on Swedish ships. In the course of the Swedish union with Norway (1814 – 1905) a canton with the symbol of this union was added to the flag; the symbol was altered in 1844. Since 1906 the flag has again been in use in its present well-known form.

SWITZERLAND
Confederation

The Swiss flag is red with a white couped cross which recalls the time of the crusades. The Swiss cantons of Uri, Schwyz and Unterwalden, after joining in the "eternal union" in 1291, did indeed use a simple red flag as their campaigning colours. In 1339, however, by which time Lucerne had also joined the confederation, a white cross on red was adopted as a common sign in the struggle for freedom against the Habsburgs, because "freedom of their own people was just as sacred as the deliverance of the Holy Land". There was also, however, a connection with medieval imperial symbolism in which the colours red and white and the cross played a great role. The Swiss have thus shown their loyalty to the Holy Roman Empire, while refusing any indirect subservience to any feudal lord. The red flag of Schwyz of 1240 was probably taken as the model and in 1289 Rudolf I of Germany added a white cross to commemorate the help of Swiss mercenaries against the Czechs. In 1815 this flag was expressly confirmed by an order of General Bachmann, and in 1848 it was declared to be the confederation flag. Its present form was defined in 1889; it is square and the length of each arm of the cross is one-sixth greater than its width. Since 1941 the merchant flag has been a rectangular version of the national flag with the proportions 2 : 3.

UNITED KINGDOM
Constitutional monarchy

The complicated pattern of the British flag, known throughout the world, dates from 1801. It took a long time to develop and reflects the dramatic history of the UK, being a combination of the flags of the patron saints of England, Scotland and Ireland. From the second half of the 13th century England used a white flag with the red cross of St George. When King James VI of Scotland became James I of England in 1603 and declared his intention to be the first monarch to be known as King of Great Britain, he ordered a flag to be devised to mark the union of the two thrones. The new flag, called the "Union Flag", was a combination of the English and Scottish flags, the latter having a blue field with the white saltire of St Andrew, the patron saint of Scotland. In order not to give priority to either flag, the field of the new flag was made blue, and the red cross of St George, edged with white, was superimposed on the white saltire of St Andrew. On 12 April 1606 James I ordered all his subjects' ships to hoist the Union Flag on the main masthead but in 1634 his successor, Charles I, confined this order to the vessels of the Royal Navy. After Charles' execution on 30 January 1649 the Scots proclaimed his son as king and this caused open enmity between England and Scotland. This Union Flag, therefore, no longer had any meaning and its use was discontinued until the monarchy was restored under Charles II in 1660, when the flag was carried once again by the king's ships. After the legislative union of England and Scotland in 1707 the Union Flag became the British flag. In 1800, under George III, the United Kingdom (i.e. of Great Britain and Ireland) came into being by the incorporation of Ireland under the Act of Union, and in 1801 the present Union Flag was created by the addition of the red saltire of St Patrick on a white field. (The cross of St Patrick was originally the arms of the Geraldines, a family of Irish-Norman origin, and it became the emblem of the Order of St Patrick in 1783.) To prevent St Patrick's cross from covering St Andrew's cross, the arms of the former were reduced in width by more than one-half and arranged so that — viewed from the centre of the flag — the red saltire is always in the left half of the white arm. The British flag has kept this pattern although the larger part of Ireland became a free state in 1922 and the official name of the UK was then changed to the United Kingdom of Great Britain and Northern Ireland.

The origin of the name "Union Jack" is uncertain. The term "Jack" was first used in the British Navy as the name for the Union Flag flown at the main masthead, the flag being a little smaller than the ensigns which ships wore at that time. It seems possible that "Jack" was used in its diminutive sense as a familiar term for this flag. The term "Union Jack" strictly applies to the Union Flag flown from the bows of a ship.

The Red Ensign was introduced in the early part of the 17th century as the ensign worn by the Red Squadron, one of three squadrons into which the Royal Navy was normally divided at that time; this ensign had St George's cross in the canton on a red field. In 1674 a royal proclamation extended to merchant ships the right to wear the Red Ensign and in 1707 the first Union Flag replaced the cross of St George in the canton. This ensign was again altered in 1801 when the present

Union Flag replaced the first in the canton (which occupies one-quarter of the flag's area) and this version was eventually confirmed in 1864 as the proper flag for merchant ships registered in the UK. In the same year the Blue Ensign was confirmed for merchant ships commanded by an officer of the Royal Naval Reserve. Both these ensigns became flags of British colonies and other dependent territories — the Red Ensign only being used in Bermuda — when the badge of the appropriate territory was added to their fly. The Blue Ensign is currently used by the following British dependencies: Gibraltar, Hong Kong, St Helena and Dependencies, British Virgin Islands, Falkland Islands and Dependencies, Cayman Islands, Montserrat, Turks and Caicos Islands, Pitcairn Islands Group and the British Antarctic Territory. Although Australia, New Zealand, Fiji and Tuvalu are all now independent, they have kept the Blue Ensign as the basis of their national flags.

VATICAN CITY STATE
Papal state

The Vatican flag has two vertical stripes, yellow and white. In the middle of the white field are crossed keys, turned outwards, representing St Peter, and the tiara from the state coat of arms. The keys suggest those referred to in Matthew 16 : 19 ("I will give you the keys of the kingdom of Heaven"), while their colours symbolize the entrusted power to admit and to open (white, representing silver) and to restrain and to bind (yellow, representing gold); the red cord by which the keys are tied together testifies that both these powers are united. The white and golden tiara — the papal triple crown — represents the Pope's threefold office of teacher, priest and shepherd. The colours correspond to the papal cockade in which red was replaced by white after the French occupation of Rome in 1808. In 1825 yellow and white were officially confirmed for the flags of the Papal States, these colours deriving both from St Peter's keys and from the arms of the kingdom of Jerusalem, which were established during the crusades and consisted of a gold cross on a silver shield. In addition, Baldwin III, King of Jerusalem (1141 − 62), used a white flag to which a yellow cross was added by his successor Amalric I (1162 − 73). The Vatican flag is square and this shape is stipulated in the basic law of 1929; from 1825 to 1870 it was the mercantile flag of the Papal States.

WEST BERLIN
Statutory city

The city flag of West Berlin consists of three horizontal stripes of red, white and red (1 : 3 : 1); on the white stripe, set slightly towards the hoist, there is a black bear rampant, with a red tongue and red claws, taken from the city coat of arms. The present city colours of Berlin were stipulated in 1861 and the flag in its present form dates from 1912; it was confirmed for West Berlin in 1954. It is similar to the flag of the capital of the GDR but differs in certain details so that the one can be distinguished from the other.

YUGOSLAVIA
Socialist federal republic

The flag consists of three horizontal stripes of blue, white and red. Over these in the centre there is a red five-pointed star edged with yellow. An imaginary circle drawn round the points of the star reaches halfway into the upper and lower stripes. The tricolour was created in 1918 out of the colours of Serbia, Croatia, Bosnia and Montenegro, and its Slavonic colours reflect those of the old Russian flag. It was officially adopted in 1921. The five-pointed star was added in accordance with the constitution in 1946 but a flag amended in this way had already been used by Yugoslav partisans from September 1941.

Dependent Territories

ÅLAND ISLANDS
Autonomous province of Finland

The Åland flag is similar to that of Sweden — a yellow Scandinavian cross on a light blue field — but it also has a narrow red cross superimposed on the yellow one. The colours reflect those of the coat of arms of Åland (blue and yellow) and that of Finland (yellow and red). The yellow cross represents the Swedish-speaking population, while the light blue colour hints at the cross of the flag of Finland of which country Åland has been part since 1917. The flag has been used since the early 1920s and was officially recognized in 1954. It may be flown on public buildings, but only side by side with the Finnish flag which must be larger.

FAEROE ISLANDS
Autonomous region of Denmark

The flag of the Faeroe Islands has a red Scandinavian cross on a white field, which are the colours of the Danish flag reversed, but the cross is additionally edged with blue. According to the ideas of the designers in 1919, white symbolizes the foaming sea and the clean, bright sky of the Faeroes, while the cross, composed of the old Faeroese colours red and blue, recalls the ties between the islands and the other Nordic countries. The flag was recognized by the local parliament in 1931, and has been used officially since 1948 when the islands became autonomous. In 1959 a lighter shade of blue was adopted. The flag may be hoisted alongside the Danish flag in any part of Denmark.

GIBRALTAR
British dependent territory

Gibraltar has two flags: the City Flag for use on land and the Blue Ensign with the colony's badge for use at sea. The City Flag is a banner of the arms granted to the city by King Ferdinand and Queen Isabella in 1502, which were confirmed as the arms of the city by the British in 1936. The City Flag has been in use for several years, but was only made official in 1982. At the same time the badge used in the fly of the Blue Ensign was altered so that it is now exactly the same as the arms. These consist of a shield divided white over red (in the proportions 2:1), charged with a castle of three towers, also in red. Hanging from the castle and lying partly on the red strip is a gold key. The motto MONTIS INSIGNIA CALPE means "the sign of Mount Calpe" (Calpe being the original name of Gibraltar) and the key refers to the colony's important position at the gateway to the Mediterranean. The shield and scroll are placed directly on the field of the Blue Ensign.

Gibraltar

GUERNSEY
British crown dependency

The flag of Guernsey has a white field charged with a red St George's cross, which is the same pattern as the English flag. It received royal approval in 1935.

ISLE OF MAN
British crown dependency
The flag is red with three legs in armour bent at the knee and joined together at the top of the thigh (following the blazon of 1968), with the feet pointing in a clockwise direction. The armour is white with gold embellishments including spurs. The device is taken from the arms of the Kings of Man in the 13th century and is of Sicilian origin. Since 1968 this flag, known as "Trinacria", has also flown on public buildings.

JAN MAYEN ISLAND
Norwegian territory
The Norwegian flag is used.

JERSEY
British crown dependency
The flag of Jersey has a white field charged with a red saltire of St Patrick. In the top triangular field there is a red shield with three gold lions passant guardant (this was granted to the island as a seal by Edward I in 1279) ensigned with the crown of the Plantagenets. In this form the flag was approved on 7 April 1981; without the arms it was used unofficially for about a hundred years.

SVALBARD
Norwegian territory
The Norwegian flag is used.

ASIA

1 CYPRUS
2 LEBANON
3 ISRAEL
4 JORDAN
5 UNITED ARAB EMIRATES
6 QATAR
7 KUWAIT
8 BAHRAIN
9 NORTH KOREA

AFGHANISTAN (1:2)

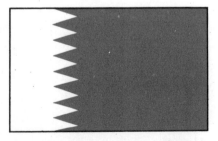

BAHRAIN (3:5)

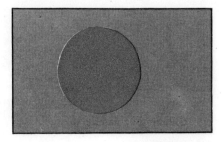

BANGLADESH (3:5)

BHUTAN (2:3)

BRUNEI (1:2)

BURMA (5:9)

CHINA (2:3)

CYPRUS (3:5)

सत्यमेव जयते

INDIA (2:3)

63

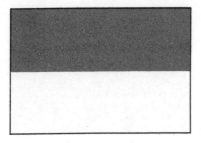

INDONESIA (2:3)

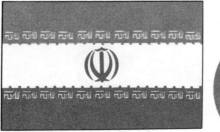

IRAN (4:7)

IRAQ (2:3)

ISRAEL (8:11)

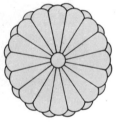

JAPAN (2:3)

JORDAN (1:2)

KAMPUCHEA (2:3)

KOREA, NORTH (1:2)

KOREA, SOUTH (2:3)

KUWAIT (1:2)

LAOS (2:3)

LEBANON (2:3)

MALAYSIA (1:2)

MALDIVES (2:3)

MONGOLIA (1:2)

NEPAL (4:3)

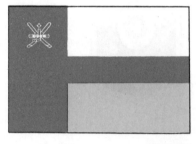

OMAN (2:3)

PAKISTAN (2:3)

PHILIPPINES(1:2)

QATAR(1:2)

SAUDI ARABIA (2:3)

SINGAPORE (2:3)

SRI LANKA (5:9)

SYRIA (2:3)

TAIWAN (2:3)

THAILAND (2:3)

TURKEY (2:3)

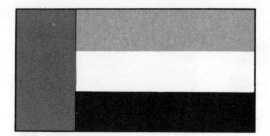

UNITED ARAB EMIRATES (1:2)

VIETNAM (2:3)

YEMEN (2:3)

SOUTH YEMEN (2:3)

77

Hong Kong (1:2)

AFGHANISTAN
Republic
The flag consists of three horizontal stripes in the traditional colours of black, red and green with the state coat of arms in the hoist of the black and red stripes. Black symbolizes the dark past of the country and at the same time represents the revolutionary Abu Muslim Khuranasi. Red is the colour of the blood shed for freedom and justice, and is also a symbol of the revolution of April 1978. Green is an old colour of Islam and also stands for the agricultural tradition of the country. The state arms have a circular field divided horizontally. In the upper white part there is a rising sun whose rays suggest the dawning of a new epoch in the country's history and the belief that after the darkness of the past a bright future is in store. In the centre of the green area there is a stylized depiction of the "minbar", a Muslim pulpit with steps leading to it, and an alcove in the wall of a mosque. Beneath the pulpit an open book represents not only the Koran and the pages of the history of the Afghan people but also enlightenment and the development of science and culture. The wreath of wheat ears stands for agriculture, the cogwheel for industry, and the five-pointed star for the hope that the revolution will ultimately be successful and that the people will find happiness. The tricolour wrapped around the lower part of the wreath repeats the colours of the flag's stripes. This flag has been in use since 1980 when it replaced a red flag with a yellow coat of arms, which was flown from 1978 to 1980. The present flag harks back to the first flag of the republic of 1974 which, however, had stripes in the proportions 1 : 1 : 2 and a different coat of arms.

BAHRAIN
Emirate
The flag is red with a white stripe in the hoist separated from the red field by eight serrations. It was introduced in this shape in about 1933 but its origin goes back to the beginning of the 19th century when it was all red, as was the custom in a number of Persian Gulf states. The white stripe is the remains of a white border, stipulated in a treaty signed with Great Britain in 1820, which indicated the country's renunciation of piracy. The present form of the flag was officially approved in 1972.

BANGLADESH
Republic within the British Commonwealth
The flag is green with a red disc which has a radius equal to one-fifth of the flag's length; in addition, the disc is offset from the centre towards the hoist by one-twentieth of the flag's length. The disc symbolizes the

newly risen sun of freedom and the blood shed during the struggle to achieve it. The green field stands for the enthusiasm of the young people and the greenness of the villages of Bangladesh, and also for the adherence of the majority of the population to Islam. The present flag dates from 1972. In 1971 the red disc had, as an additional charge, a yellow outline map of the country.

BHUTAN
Kingdom
The flag of Bhutan is divided diagonally from the bottom of the hoist to the top of the fly, into two triangles in the traditional Chinese colours of saffron yellow in the hoist and orange-red in the fly. Over the dividing line there is the white Bhutanese wingless dragon outlined in black. The dragon faces to the right, and holds balls representing the eggs of cognizance and the universe. Saffron represents the king's authority and his leading role in directing both religious and worldly affairs; red reflects the spiritual power of Buddhism which is represented by two sects in the country. Originally the red part of the flag was brown, but in the 1960s it was changed to its present shade. The dragon has various symbolical functions — the Tibetan name for Bhutan,"Druk-Yul", can be translated as "Land of the Dragon" — and the thunder in the valleys of Bhutan is said to announce the dragon's presence. The flag clearly derives from the old Chinese flags and recalls the country's former links with China in general. The present pattern of the flag appeared in 1971.

BRUNEI
Sultanate
A yellow flag with a diagonal stripe, divided white over black with the proportions 17:15, was introduced in 1906. In 1959 the red coat of arms of Brunei, which has been in official use since 1932, was placed in the centre of the flag. This coat of arms consists of two free standing, upraised human arms with a crescent placed between them; within the horns of the crescent there is a winged support with a small flag, and beneath the crescent there is a scroll. The yellow Arabic inscription on the crescent reads: "Always render service by God's guidance", while the inscription on the scroll says: "Brunei, abode of peace". Yellow is the sultan's colour, white belonged to the first wazir (minister), and black to another wazir of the country. These are typical Malaysian princely colours of rank.

BURMA
Republic
The Burmese flag is red with a blue canton charged with a white cogwheel with fourteen cogs, in the centre of which are two ears of rice. The wheel is surrounded by fourteen white five-pointed stars, one against

each cog. These stars represent the fourteen states and provinces of the Union of Burma. The cogwheel and the two ears of rice symbolize the indissoluble union of the workers and the peasants. Red and white recall the colours of the flag of the resistance movement during World War II, the Anti-Fascist People's Freedom League. Red stands for gallantry, white for purity and honour, and blue for peace and endurance. The flag in this form was introduced early in 1974; previously (since 1947) the canton had been charged with a large white five-pointed star surrounded by five similar smaller stars.

CHINA
People's republic
The flag features the traditional Chinese colours and was inspired by the Soviet flag. It has a red field and in the upper hoist there is a large yellow five-pointed star with four smaller yellow stars. These are arranged so that one of their points is directed towards the centre of the large star. According to the official interpretation, the large star represents the common programme and the unity of the people led by the Communist Party, while the smaller stars stand for the workers, the peasants, the petty bourgeoisie and the patriotic capitalists, all of whom participate in the common programme of building socialism. Red is the colour of revolution but in the past it symbolized the Chinese people. The flag was introduced in 1949.

CYPRUS
Republic within the British Commonwealth
The white flag bears a copper-coloured map of Cyprus (the name is derived from the Greek word for copper) above two crossed olive branches which are a symbol of the longing for peace and conciliation between the Greek and Turkish inhabitants of the island. White is the colour of peace and copper can be taken to represent the island's wealth of copper deposits. The flag was introduced in 1960 after an agreement in 1959 which stipulated that the design must be neutral and the colours must not represent either the Greek or the Turkish population of the island.

INDIA
Federal republic within the British Commonwealth
After the Congress Party had led India to independence in 1947, India adopted as her state flag a slightly amended version of the flag which the Congress Party had used since 1933. The Indian flag consists of three horizontal stripes, saffron, white and green; in the centre of the white stripe there is a blue drawing of Emperor Asoka's "dharma chakra" ("wheel of life") which was discovered in the excavations of Sarnath in the Indus valley. The "chakra" is a symbol of Indian culture and it is also part of the state coat of arms. Saffron symbolizes courage and

sacrifice, white stands for peace and truth, and green for faith and chivalry. According to another interpretation these colours symbolize natural wealth, maintenance of life, and production, while the "chakra" has to bring these three elements into successful working order. The twenty-four rays of the wheel stand for the hours of the day, the endless course of life, and progress; blue is a reference to the sky and the sea. The "chakra" is also an ancient sign of Brahmanism, a symbol of the sun and an attribute of its god Vishnu.

INDONESIA
Republic
The red-and-white flag is said to have flown from 1293 to 1475 in the Majapahit Empire. Its colours were easy to obtain among the materials at hand — white cotton cloth and red pigment from salt-water molluscs. The colours also represent those concepts which come in pairs: sky and earth, gallantry and purity, and freedom and justice. In 1922 the flag became a symbol of the partisans fighting against Dutch occupation; in 1945 and again in 1949 it was declared to be the national flag. Apart from its proportions the flag is identical with that of Monaco.

IRAN
Republic
The flag consists of three horizontal stripes in the traditional Iranian colours of green, white and red but the white stripe is somewhat wider than the other two, and projects into them by narrow rectangular indentations. The lower edge of the green stripe and the upper edge of the red one are each charged with the inscription "Allah-o-Akbar" ("God is Great"), repeated eleven times in white stylized Kufi script. The Iranian coat of arms in red is carried in the centre of the white stripe and comprises four crescents arranged symmetrically with two on either side of a vertical sword-blade with a stress mark called "tashdid" above it. The emblem is a symbolic representation of Allah and a demonstration of man's growth and evolution towards Allah. The five main elements of the arms are symbolical of the five principles of Islam, and their vertical positioning suggests the road to the only Allah. The four crescents signify the four phases of the moon, symbolizing the growth of the Islamic faith. The sword stands for strength and gallantry and this is reinforced by the "tashdid". The shape of the arms also recalls that of the globe. The flag's red stripe stands for revolution, white is for peace and green for Islam. The twenty-two repetitions of the inscription at the edges of the coloured stripes commemorate 22 Bahman 1357 (11 February 1979) which is celebrated as the day of victory of the Iranian revolution. Although Iran was proclaimed a republic on 1 April 1979, the new Iranian flag was not confirmed by parliament until 29 July 1980. Prior to that date the Iranian tricolour without the imperial lion, or with the lion but without the imperial crown, was in use.

IRAQ
Republic
The flag dates from 1963 when a union between Iraq, Egypt and Syria was expected. That is why it follows the basic Egyptian pattern of three horizontal stripes coloured red, white and black. The white stripe contains three green five-pointed stars which represent the three above-mentioned countries. The flag remains unchanged although the federation did not come into being. The same pattern was also used for the flag of Syria from 1963 until 1971 (only the proportions were 1 : 2). Red stands for gallantry in battle, white for magnanimity, and black for the Muslim victories of the past; green is the colour of Islam.

ISRAEL
Republic
The flag is white with two blue horizontal stripes near the upper and lower edges of the flag (the proportions are 14 : 30 : 85 : 30 : 14), and there is a blue six-pointed Shield of David in the centre. The hexagram, formed by two overlapping triangles, is a traditional Jewish symbol. White and blue are the colours of Jewish ritual cloths, and in their new interpretation they stand for the purity of Zionist ideals and for the sky. The flag was officially adopted in 1948, and was based on the flag introduced by Zionists in 1891; this flag was approved following its submission at the World Zionist Organization congress in Basle in 1897.

JAPAN
Empire
The flag is called "Hi-no-maru" ("the sun disc") and was originally used by the shoguns (military dictators) of the House of Tokugawa. In 1854 it became the national marine flag and was confirmed by law as the national flag in 1870. It is white with a red disc which is usually placed in the centre of the flag, although sometimes it is set slightly towards the hoist. White is a traditional Japanese colour and expresses purity and honesty, while the red disc is a symbol of the sun and denotes passion, sincerity and enthusiasm.

JORDAN
Kingdom
The Jordanian flag consists of three horizontal stripes — black, white, and green — with a red triangle in the hoist reaching to almost one-half of the flag's length, charged with a white seven-pointed star. These are the so-called pan-Arab colours derived in 1921 from the flag of Hejaz. The first emir of Jordan (then called Transjordan), Abdullah, was a son of King Hussein of Hejaz and consequently adopted the Hejaz flag. (Each member of the pan-Arab federation which was then being prepared had to add one or more stars to a similar flag.) Black is the colour of the Abbasids, white of the Umayyads, green of the Fatimids, and red of the

Hashemites — the house to which the King of Hejaz belonged. The seven points of the star represent the first seven verses of the Koran.

KAMPUCHEA
Republic
The flag has the traditional red colour and in its centre features a yellow silhouette of five pointed towers with two steps at either side; this is regarded as a representation of the famous temple Angkor Wat built in the 12th century. Created in 1950 as the flag of the Khmer Liberation Front, it was taken over in 1978 by the National United Front for the Salvation of Kampuchea. Red symbolizes the sincere hope of the people for a happy future, and yellow represents Kampuchean traditions. The towers stand for the five prerequisites of public life in Kampuchea: peace, independence, democracy, neutrality and non-alignment of the country while on the path to socialism. Care should be taken not to confuse this flag with a similar flag of Democratic Kampuchea (1975 — 79) on which Angkor Wat was pictured with three cupolas.

KOREA, DEMOCRATIC PEOPLE'S REPUBLIC OF (NORTH)
People's democratic republic
The flag created in 1948 consists of three stripes — blue, red, blue — separated from each other by two narrow white lines, the proportions being 6 : 2 : 17 : 2 : 6. The hoist of the red stripe is charged with a white disc containing a red five-pointed star. The blue stripes stand for the people's desire for peace, the red one symbolizes the revolutionary spirit of the struggle for socialism, and white — a traditional Korean colour — reoresents the purity of the ideals of (North) Korea and national sovereignty. The five-pointed star signifies the happy prospects of the people building socialism under the leadership of the Korean Workers' Party. The white disc suggests the yin and yang symbol ("t'aeguk" in Korean) in the flag of the Republic of Korea.

KOREA, REPUBLIC OF (SOUTH)
Republic
The flag dates from 1882 — 3, when Korea was an independent, united kingdom, and was reintroduced in (South) Korea in 1950. It consists of a white field charged with a circular red-and-blue pictograph, the yin and yang symbol ("t'aeguk" in Korean), expressing the fundamental credo of Buddhist philosophy, which derives from the well-known union of opposites. The "t'aeguk", which also appears in the coat of arms of South Korea, represents absoluteness; its red and blue components represent fundamental pairs of opposites such as spirit and matter, good and evil, day and night, male and female, life and death, and positive and negative. The four black trigrams (sets of three broken and unbroken parallel lines known as "kwae") are cult signs denoting the sky, summer and the south (upper left), the moon, autumn and the west (upper

right), the earth, winter and the north (bottom left) and the sun, spring and the east (bottom right). White is a traditional Korean colour and symbolizes peace; red is at the opposite end of the spectrum from blue.

KUWAIT
Emirate
The pan-Arab colours of this flag are arranged in three horizontal stripes of green, white and red, and in the hoist there is a black trapezium. The symbolism of the colours is officially explained in this way: white signifies deeds, black — battlefields, green — meadows, and red, soaked with the blood of our enemies — the future. Another explanation says that white signifies honour, black stands for the sand whirled by Kuwaiti horsemen in the battles for freedom, green for the fields and red for gallantry. The flag was introduced in 1961.

LAOS
People's democratic republic
After liberation in 1975, the flag of the Patriotic Front of Laos (Neo Lao Istala), generally called Pathet Lao abroad, was accepted as the national flag. It has three horizontal stripes (in the proportions 1 : 2 : 1) coloured red, dark blue and red. In the centre of the blue stripe there is a white disc of which the diameter is one-third of the flag's width and four-fifths of the width of the blue stripe. Red symbolizes the heart of the Laotian people and their blood shed for independence, blue stands for their well-being, and white for the country's future and for justice which the people now enjoy. The white disc also suggests the full moon, an old symbol of happiness and welfare. The flag was already in existence in 1945 when the revolutionary forces declared Laos independent, but in 1947 the feudal kingdom adopted a red flag with three white elephants. It was not until 1975 that the flag of 1945 became an official state symbol.

LEBANON
Republic
The flag has three horizontal stripes of red, white and red in the proportions 1 : 2 : 1. In the middle of the white stripe there is a green cedar of Lebanon with a brown trunk, an ancient symbol of the country and of strength, holiness and immortality. As early as in the 18th and 19th centuries the Maronite Christians of Lebanon used a white flag with a green cedar. Red represents self-sacrifice and white stands for peace. According to another interpretation red is the colour of the Qaysites and white of the Yamanites, these being the two tribes who were continually at odds on Lebanese territory from 634 until 1711. The flag was created in 1943; prior to this the French tricolour with a cedar in the centre had been in use since 1920.

MALAYSIA
Federation within the British Commonwealth
The Malaysian flag was inspired by the flag of the USA both in pattern and symbolism. The fourteen horizontal stripes, seven red and seven white, represent the thirteen member states of the federation and the territory of its capital, and there are also fourteen rays of the yellow star which, together with a yellow crescent, appears in the blue canton. The height of the canton is that of eight stripes. Red and white are favourite colours in the countries of south-east Asia; blue, which is taken from the British flag, commemorates the link with the British Commonwealth; and yellow — the royal colour — represents the sultans of the nine sultanates of the federation. The crescent and star are symbols of Islam. The flag in this form dates from 1963; from 1950 it had had eleven stripes and an eleven-pointed star and crescent in the canton.

MALDIVES
Republic within the British Commonwealth
The flag is green with a broad red border and a white crescent in the middle. Green is the colour of peace, progress and Islam, and red recalls the blood shed for freedom; the crescent is a symbol of Islam. The flag in this form has been used since independence was gained in 1965. Between 1953 and 1965, when the Maldives were an autonomous sultanate, there was also a narrow border of white and black diagonal stripes in the hoist. As recently as in the first quarter of the 20th century the flag of the Maldives was all red, just like the flags of several other maritime Arab countries, and only later was the green field with the white crescent added.

MONGOLIA
People's democratic republic
The flag consists of three vertical stripes — red, light blue and red; the red stripe in the hoist is charged with a yellow ideogram, called the "soyombo" and topped with a yellow five-pointed star which is the symbol of socialism and the bright future of the country. Each component of the "soyombo" has its own symbolical meaning. The uppermost figure represents fire, in turn symbolizing happiness and contentment. Its three flames signify the past, the present and the future. The sun and moon give the idea of the universe and eternity (the young moon is taken to be the father of Mongolia and the golden sun her mother). Next a triangle, which is repeated at the foot of the ideogram, symbolizes an arrow and a spear pointing towards the ground, which in Mongolian heraldry signifies death to the enemy. The narrow rectangle, again repeated further down, recalls flat steppe country, straightforwardness, justice and honesty. In the centre of the emblem there is the ancient Buddhist yin and yang symbol of the union of opposites (such as fire and water, earth and sky, male and female), looking like the bodies

of two fish arranged to form a circular motif. A fish which never closes its eyes while asleep denotes watchfulness and vigilance. Two tall rectangles, one on each side, represent pillars, strength, hardness, and the proverb that "two friends are stronger than a stone wall". The yellow colour denotes gold and its stability, even when put to the test of fire; blue is a traditional Mongolian colour and also stands for the cloudless sky; and red is not only the symbol of revolution but also of love and victory. The flag was introduced in 1940.

NEPAL
Kingdom
This flag, quite exceptional in shape, is composed of two crimson blue-edged triangles of unequal height placed one above the other (originally these were two pennants flown together which merged into one flag about a hundred years ago). The upper triangle bears a stylized white moon in outline and the lower one bears the sun, these being the symbols of Buddhism (in 1962 their facial features were deleted) and of the eternal course of time. The picture of the moon represents the royal family while the sun stands for the Rana family, whose regime lasted until 1951. The indentations of the flag also recall the towering Himalaya Mountains in which Nepal is situated. The flag can, however, also be interpreted as expressing the wish that the country will exist as long as the sun and the moon. Its present form dates from 1962. The combination of crimson and blue is typical of Nepalese religious and secular art, crimson being a traditional Nepalese colour.

OMAN
Sultanate
The flag has three horizontal stripes of white, red and green (in the proportions 2:1:2) with a red vertical stripe in the hoist. The width of the vertical stripe is half that of the flag's width. In the upper hoist there is the state coat of arms in white with details in red. The arms consist of two crossed curved sabres in richly decorated sheaths, a dagger (known as the "gambia") and a fastener. The overriding red colour denotes that the majority of the population belong to the Islamic Kharijites (the previous flag was all red); red is also associated with the ruler and with Muscat. White is the colour of peace, of Oman and of the imam (the religious authority in the country), while green represents Djebel Akhdar (Green Mountain) ridge and Islam. The flag was introduced in 1970.

PAKISTAN
Republic
The national flag was created in 1947 and was based on the flag of the All-Indian Muslim League, which had been in use since 1906. The

green field bears the symbols of Islam, a white crescent and a white five-pointed star which is positioned towards the upper fly of the flag. A white vertical stripe occupying one-quarter of the flag's length was added to represent the Hindus, Christians, Buddhists, Parsees and other religious minorities, thus suggesting religious tolerance, while green is the colour of Islam. In 1964 the individual components were attributed with the following symbolism: green — prosperity, white — peace, the crescent — progress, the star — light and knowledge. The green colour is designated officially as "tartan green".

PHILIPPINES
Republic
The flag consists of two horizontal stripes, blue over red, with a white triangle inserted in the hoist. In the centre of the triangle there is a yellow sun with eight triple rays and in each corner of the triangle there is a yellow five-pointed star placed so that in each case one of its points is directed towards the adjacent corner of the triangle. Red stands for courage and gallantry, blue for high ideals and white for peace and purity. The sun signifies the light of freedom and justice; it is the symbol of the republic because its eight rays honour the eight provinces which rose up in 1898 against Spanish rule. The three yellow stars represent the principal islands, Luzon and Mindanao, and the Visayan Islands, while the white equilateral triangle symbolizes equality, recalling the revolutionary organization called the Katipunan which led the anti-Spanish revolution. The Philippine flag has one special feature — when the country is at war, the flag is hoisted upside down so that blue is at the bottom.

QUATAR
Emirate
The flag is maroon with a white stripe in the hoist separated from the brown field by nine serrations. Originally the flag was red, as was common in a number of Persian Gulf states. The white stripe was added in about 1855 to indicate that the country had renounced piracy. In 1949 the red colour was replaced by maroon in order to distinguish the flag from that of Bahrain and other similar flags of some of the then Trucial States (now known as the United Arab Emirates). It is said that another reason for this change was the ease with which the natural dye used in Qatar turns maroon when exposed to the sun. Until 1960 the Arabic name of the country in white was also placed on the flag together with a row of small white diamond shapes. The serration between the two colours is of a purely decorative nature.

SAUDI ARABIA
Kingdom
The flag is green with a white Arabic inscription and a sword with a straight blade. Green is the colour of Islam, Muhammad and the Fati-

mids, a dynasty tracing its descent from the Prophet's daughter Fatima. The sword symbolizes the gains of Islam and the military successes of the puritan Wahhabis. Above the sword is the Muslim credo: "There is no God but Allah, and Muhammad is his Prophet". This text occupies a rectangle which is half as long as the flag while the height of the rectangle is just one-quarter of the flag's width; the inscription reads from right to left on both sides of the flag. There have been various arrangements of the flag since the beginning of the 19th century: from 1946 it had two crossed swords and, later on, there was one sword with a curved blade beneath the inscription while the flag with two swords was reserved for the king. The present form dates from 1973.

SINGAPORE
Republic within the British Commonwealth
The flag consists of two horizontal stripes in the Malaysian colours of red and white. In the hoist of the red stripe there is a white crescent together with five small white five-pointed stars forming the shape of an imaginary pentagon. The crescent stands for the young state and the five stars represent the ideals of democracy, peace, progress, justice and equality. Red symbolizes brotherhood and equality between men, and white stands for purity and virtue. The flag dates from 1959.

SRI LANKA
Republic within the British Commonwealth
The basis of the present flag is a yellow-edged, dark red field with a yellow lion holding a sword as a symbol of power. This ancient flag of the kings of Kandy was adopted in 1948. In 1951 two vertical stripes, green and orange, with a yellow border around them were added in the hoist. Green represents the Muslims (7 per cent of the population) and orange stands for the Hindu Tamils (18 per cent), these two groups being the national minorities alongside the 74 per cent of Sinhalese. In 1972 stylized leaves replaced silhouettes of a Buddhist pagoda in the corners of the red rectangle and in 1978 they were in turn replaced by realistic drawings. The leaves are those of the sacred pipul tree("Ficus religiosa") under which Gautama meditated and is supposed to have received enlightenment, thus becoming the Buddha. Yellow symbolizes the protection of the country and the people, afforded by Buddhism. The lion is an ancient symbol of the island and recalls that the Aryan mythical ruler and conqueror of the island, Vijaya, was a lion, its native name, "sinha", being the basis of the original name of the island, "Sinhala dvipa" (Lions' Island).

SYRIA
Republic
The Syrian flag consists of three horizontal stripes — red, white and black — with two green five-pointed stars in the white stripe. Red sym-

bolizes the struggle and sacrifices for freedom, white signifies peace, and black stands for the dark colonial past. At the time of the creation of the flag in 1958, the two stars represented the Syrian and Egyptian regions of the then United Arab Republic which the two countries formed (1958−61). After the disintegration of the UAR, for two years Syria used her old flag of 1932−58 (horizontal stripes of green, white and black, with three red five-pointed stars). From 1963 until 1971, when a union with Iraq and Egypt was contemplated, the red-white-black tricolour was in use once again but this time it had three green stars in the white stripe (see Iraq, p. 64). After joining Egypt and Libya to form the Federation of Arab Republics in 1972, the three stars were replaced by the arms of the Federation. In protest against the policy of the Egyptian leadership towards Israel, however, Syria renounced this flag and on 30 March 1980 returned to the flag of 1958−61.

TAIWAN
Republic
Taiwan is the territory controlled since 1949 by the Republic of China ("Nationalist China"), and uses the flag adopted in 1928 as the national flag of China. The flag was first used as a military ensign in 1914, and is based on the flag of the ruling Kuomintang party. It is known as the "White Sun in Blue Sky on Red Field". The sun has twelve rays which stand for the twelve two-hour periods of the day, and the sun itself represents the yang or male element in the well-known yin and yang principle. The colours are said to stand for the Three Principles of the People, laid down by the father of the Chinese Revolution of 1911, Dr Sun Yat-sen: popular well-being, popular government and popular sovereignty. However, as in the People's Republic of China, the red field undoubtedly stands for the Chinese people themselves, in this case guided by the White Sun in Blue Sky flag of the Kuomintang.

THAILAND
Kingdom
Although Thailand has in the past been called the "land of the white elephant", there has been no elephant pictured on the Thai flag (except on the naval ensign) since 1917. In the previous year the flag was modified by the insertion of a horizontal white stripe above and below the elephant but in 1917 the elephant was omitted. In the same year the country was involved in a war and because the flags of almost all the allies, but especially France, contained red, white and blue, the space between the two white stripes was made blue. In this way a tricolour ("Trairong")with stripes of red, white, blue, white and red (in the proportions 1 : 1 : 2 : 1 : 1) was created. Blue is the Thai national colour and represents royalty, white stands for Buddhism and the purity of the nation, and red symbolizes freedom and the blood shed in achieving it.

TURKEY
Republic
The present pattern of the Turkish flag dates from 1844. It is red with a white crescent and a white five-pointed star, both being long-established symbols of Islam; a crescent appeared on the Osmanli flag as early as in the 16th century, and a star (six-pointed) was added in 1793. One of the points of the star touches the imaginary line connecting the two horns of the crescent, and the whole emblem is placed slightly towards the hoist. From 1920 until 1923 the basic colour of the flag was green. According to a regulation of 1936 and a law of 1937, the Turkish flag ought to have a narrow white stripe in the hoist (one-thirtieth of the flag's width) but it is not the accepted practice for it to appear. The Turkish flag served as the model for the flag of Tunisia.

UNITED ARAB EMIRATES
Federation of emirates
The flag has three horizontal stripes, green, white and black, with a red vertical stripe in the hoist, the width of the red stripe being a quarter of the length of the flag. The flag itself is a new arrangement of the recognized pan-Arab colours and was created in 1971.

VIETNAM
Socialist republic
The red field of the flag bears a yellow five-pointed star which symbolizes the unity of the people and the building of socialism; its five points represent the Vietnamese workers, peasants, intellectuals, youth and soldiers. It has the symbolism of a red star but since the field of the flag is red, yellow was chosen for it instead (red and yellow are favourite colours in this part of the world). The colour of the flag signifies revolution and the blood shed for the freedom of the country. The form of the flag dates from about 1940 and several variations were used during the struggle against the French from 1945. The star, drawn within an imaginary circle with a radius equalling one-fifth of the flag's length, originally had shorter points until the present shape was adopted in 1955.

YEMEN ARAB REPUBLIC
Republic
The flag displays the pan-Arab colours, following the Egyptian pattern, in three horizontal stripes — red, white and black — with a green five-pointed star in the centre. Red symbolizes revolution, white represents purity and the hope for a better future, and black stands for the dark period of the imam's rule in Yemen. The green star signifies unity and independence, and the fertile land and the well-being of the republic. The flag was introduced in 1962.

YEMEN PEOPLE'S DEMOCRATIC REPUBLIC (SOUTH YEMEN)
People's democratic republic

The national flag was created in 1967 and was based on the flag of the National Liberation Front. It has horizontal stripes in the pan-Arab colours of red, white and black with a light-blue isosceles triangle charged with a red five-pointed star based on the hoist. The star is placed so that one of its points is directed towards the apex of the blue triangle. Red is the colour of revolution, white is that of peace, and black represents delivery from colonial oppression. The blue triangle stands for the people, the red star for the National Liberation Front.

Dependent Territories

BRITISH INDIAN OCEAN TERRITORY
British dependent territory

The British flag is used.

CHRISTMAS ISLAND
Australian overseas territory

The Australian flag is used.

COCOS ISLANDS
Australian overseas territory

The Australian flag is used.

HONG KONG
British dependent territory

The Blue Ensign with the badge of Hong Kong is used. This badge is the coat of arms of the colony, granted in 1959, placed in a white circle in the fly of the flag. The shield is silver with blue and white wavy stripes at the bottom representing the sea, and two junks; a red embattled chief is charged with a golden naval coronet. The name "Hong Kong" appears on a scroll beneath the shield which is supported by a British lion and a Chinese dragon, both standing on a green mound lapped by waves. The crest above the shield shows a crowned British lion holding a pearl. The flag in this form was introduced in 1959.

MACAO
Portuguese autonomous overseas territory

The Portuguese flag is used.

AFRICA

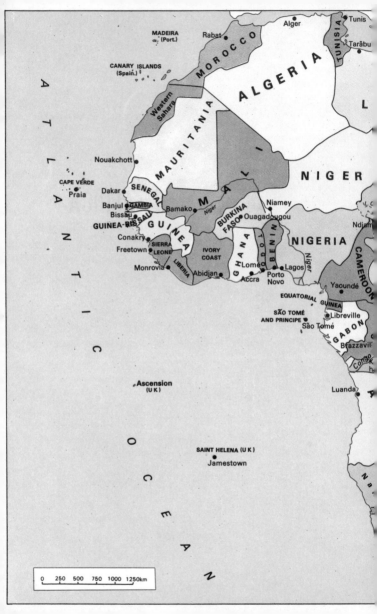

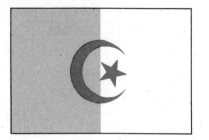

ALGERIA (2:3)

ANGOLA (2:3)

BENIN (2:3)

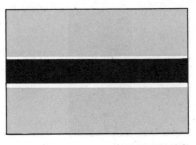

BOTSWANA (2:3)

BURKINA FASO (2:3)

BURUNDI (2:3)

CAMEROON (2:3)

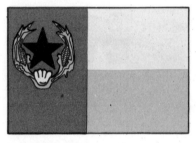

CAPE VERDE (2:3)

CENTRAL AFRICAN REPUBLIC (3:5)

98

CHAD (2:3)

COMOROS (3:5)

CONGO (2:3)

DJIBOUTI (21:38)

EGYPT (2:3)

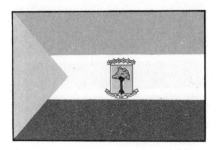

EQUATORIAL GUINEA (5:8)

ETHIOPIA (2:3)

GABON (3:4)

101

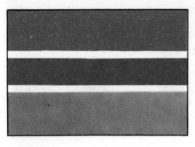

GAMBIA (2:3)

GHANA (2:3)

GUINEA (2:3)

GUINEA-BISSAU (1:2)

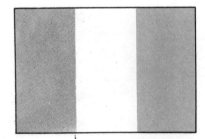

IVORY COAST (2:3)

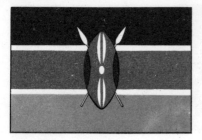

KENYA (2:3)

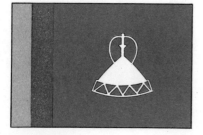

LESOTHO (2:3)

LIBERIA (10:19)

LIBYA (1:2)

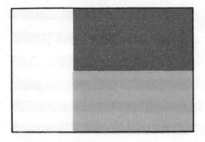

MADAGASCAR (2:3)

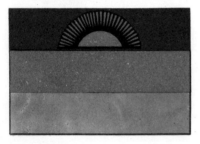

MALAWI (2:3)

MALI (2:3)

MAURITANIA (2:3)

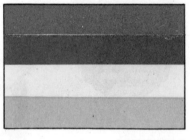

MAURITIUS (2:3)

MOROCCO (2:3)

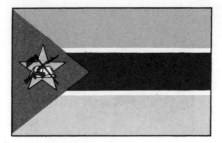

MOZAMBIQUE (3:5)

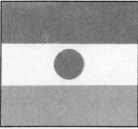

NIGER (6:7)

NIGERIA (1:2)

RWANDA (2:3)

SÃO TOMÉ AND PRÍNCIPE (1:2)

SENEGAL (2:3)

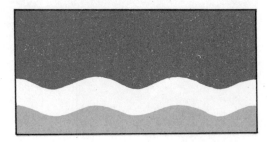

SEYCHELLES (1:2)

SIERRA LEONE (2:3)

SOMALIA (2:3)

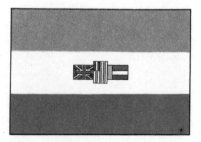

SOUTH AFRICA (2:3)

SUDAN (1:2)

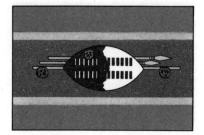

SWAZILAND (2:3)

TANZANIA (2:3)

TOGO (2:3)

TUNISIA (2:3)

UGANDA (2:3)

ZAÏRE (2:3)

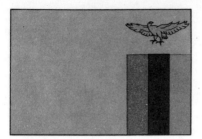

ZAMBIA (2:3)

ZIMBABWE (1:2)

Azores (2:3)

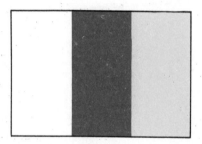

Canary Islands (2:3)

Madeira (2:3)

St. Helena (1:2)

ALGERIA
Republic
The flag of Algeria consists of two vertical stripes, green and white, with a red crescent and a five-pointed star in its centre, the star positioned so that two of its points touch the edge of the green stripe. The crescent and star are symbols of Islam; the Algerian crescent, however, has longer horns than those usually found in the flags of other Muslim countries and in Algeria this signifies good fortune. Green is the colour of Islam; white symbolizes purity; and red stands for freedom. The flag probably appeared for the first time during the anti-French demonstrations in 1928. From 1954 it was a symbol of the war for national liberation and from 1958 it flew as the flag of the provisional government; in 1962 it became the national flag.

ANGOLA
People's republic
The flag has two horizontal stripes, red over black; in its centre there is a yellow emblem consisting of half a cogwheel (with nine cogs), a machete and a five-pointed star. Red is the colour of the blood of the Angolans shed during colonial oppression, in the struggle for national liberation and in the revolution. The black stripe symbolizes the African continent, while the yellow colour represents the wealth of the country. The cogwheel stands for the working class and industrial production, the machete for the peasants, agricultural production and armed struggle for freedom, while the star signifies internationalism and progress which derive from the unity of the workers in industry and agriculture. The five points of the star represent unity, freedom, justice, democracy and progress. The flag originates from that of the Popular Movement for the Liberation of Angola (MPLA), and was introduced in 1975.

BENIN
Republic
The flag of Benin, formerly Dahomey, is green and in its upper hoist there is a red five-pointed star in the centre of an imaginary square with sides one-third that of the flag's width. Green is the symbol of agriculture and red stands for revolution. The star represents the national unity of all the revolutionary forces and the victory over the enemy within and without, so that a new, revolutionary and socialist Benin nation could be born. The flag was introduced in 1975 when the present name of the country was adopted. From 1959 the flag of Dahomey had been used.

BOTSWANA
Republic within the British Commonwealth
The field of the flag is blue with a black horizontal stripe in the middle, edged with two narrow white stripes (the proportions being $9:1:4:1:9$). This represents the coexistence of the black and the white members of the population under the blue African skies. (Blue also symbolizes water which is vital throughout the whole country.) The flag was created in 1966.

BURKINA FASO
Republic
The flag consists of two equal horizontal stripes, red over green, with a yellow, five-pointed star in the centre, and thus includes the pan-African colours (red, yellow and green). It was created in 1984 when the then Republic of Upper Volta changed its name and symbols of sovereignty, to indicate a fresh stage in the decolonialization of the country. Previously (1959 — 84) a flag with three horizontal stripes — black, white and red — was used.

BURUNDI
Republic
The field of the flag is divided by a white saltire into four triangles, those in the hoist and the fly being green, and the top and bottom ones red. In the centre there is a white circle with three red six-pointed stars, edged with green, forming a triangle. These stars symbolize the words in the national motto — Unity, Work, Progress — in the state coat of arms and they also represent the three ethnic groups of the country — the Tutsi, Hutu and Twa. The red colour stands for the sacrifices during the struggle for freedom, green for progress and hope, and white for peace. The flag dates from 1966 when the country was proclaimed a republic. From 1962 until September 1966 the circle in the centre of the flag bore the royal drum and a sorghum plant, and from September until November 1966 the sorghum alone.

CAMEROON
Republic
The flag of Cameroon is a tricolour with vertical stripes in the pan-African colours — green, red and yellow — with a yellow five-pointed star in the centre of the red stripe. Green denotes the rich forest vegetation of the southern part of the country, and the hope for a happy future; red is the symbol of independence and unity; and yellow stands for the savannas in the northern part of the country and for the sun as the source of the nation's happiness. The star symbolizes the unity of the country. Originally, since 1957, Cameroon had used the basic tricolour (after Ghana, Cameroon was the second modern

African state to adopt the pan-African colours). In 1961 two small yellow five-pointed stars were added to the flag, placed one above the other in the upper part of the green stripe (as symbols of the two territorial divisions of the Cameroonian federation which lasted until 1972). The present form of the flag dates from 1975.

CAPE VERDE
Republic
The national flag is derived — as is that of Guinea-Bissau — from the flag of the African Party for the Independence of Guinea and Cape Verde (PAIGC). It consists of two horizontal stripes — yellow over green — with a vertical red stripe in the hoist. Just above the middle of this stripe there is an emblem dominated by a black five-pointed star. This is flanked by a wreath formed by two stalks of maize (with ears) joined at the bottom by a sea shell. The maize stalks and leaves are green with yellow outlines, the ears are yellow with criss-crossed brown lines, and the husks are light green. The sea shell is yellow. Black stands for the independent African nation, while the maize stalks are for the country's crops and the sea shell for the food from the sea. Red symbolizes the blood of the martyrs and heroes who led the country to independence; yellow represents the prosperity of the people and the results of their labour; while green stands for hope and the lush tropical vegetation. The flag has been in use since 1975.

CENTRAL AFRICAN REPUBLIC
Republic
The basis of the unusual flag of this country is a combination of the pan-African colours of yellow, green and red with the colours of the French tricolour, resulting in four horizontal stripes of blue, white, green and yellow, and overall in the centre a vertical red stripe with the same width as the others. In the upper hoist, in the blue stripe, there is a yellow five-pointed star of independence, representing African unity. The flag contains the national colours of all the countries of what was formerly French Equatorial Africa (Ubangi-Shari, Chad, Gabon and Congo). Ubangi-Shari became independent as the Central African Republic in August 1960. According to one interpretation, blue symbolizes the African population, white stands for the white Europeans, green is for the mulattos, yellow for the Asians, and red for the blood of people of all colours, which represents the hope that all races will eventually live in harmony. The flag was introduced in 1958 and was not even changed during 1976 — 9 when the country was proclaimed an empire.

CHAD
Republic
The blue-yellow-red tricolour was based on the French pattern but only two of the pan-African colours were used, blue replacing green.

Blue recalls the sky, hope, agriculture, the fertile southern part of the country and her rivers; yellow stands for the sun and the northern part of the country which is a desert; and red signifies progress, unity and the readiness of the people to sacrifice themselves for their country. The flag was introduced in 1959.

COMOROS
Republic

The flag of the Comoros is green with a white crescent and four white five-pointed stars between the horns of the crescent, which is placed centrally and turned towards the lower fly. The colour green and the crescent are symbols of Islam, and the four stars represent the four main islands of Grande-Comore (Njazidja), Anjouan (Nzwani), Mohéli (Mwali) and Mayotte (Mahoré), thus emphasizing the unity of the country (although Mayotte, with its Catholic inhabitants, is administered by France as one of her overseas territories). The flag was introduced in 1978 and resembles the flag which was used from 1963 until 1975. The flag flown from 1975, when the Comoros joined the United Nations, until 1978 had two horizontal stripes, red over green (in the proportions 2 : 1), with the crescent and the stars in the upper hoist.

CONGO
Republic

The Congolese flag is red with the state emblem in the upper hoist; the emblem consists of a crossed hammer and hoe under a yellow five-pointed star, flanked by two curved green palm branches. Red is a symbol of the struggle of the Congolese people for freedom during the colonial era. The star stands for hope, the green branches for peace, and the hammer and hoe represent the workers and the peasants united in the building of the new state. Although red is the dominant colour, the flag of the Congo contains all three pan-African colours. It was introduced in 1969.

DJIBOUTI
Republic

On the day of the proclamation of independence, 27 June 1977, the flag of the organization for national liberation — the People's African League for Independence (LPAI) — became the national flag of this small country. The flag consists of two horizontal stripes, light blue over light green, with a white equilateral triangle based on the hoist; in the centre of the triangle there is a red five-pointed star. Blue represents the sea and the sky, and also the Issas who form the majority of the population; green stands for the green countryside and the Afars; white signifies peace; and red recalls the struggle for independence and expresses hope for a happy future for the country. Red also emphasizes the unity between the Afars and the Issas which intensified during the bloody struggle to attain equality, symbolized by the equilateral triangle.

EGYPT
Republic
The flag consists of three horizontal stripes — red, white and black — and in the centre there is the national emblem, a golden eagle facing the hoist. The eagle is charged with an escutcheon on its breast and holds in its claws a scroll with the name of the country, Arab Republic of Egypt, written in Arabic. The national emblem is all in gold on the flag, although for other uses it is fully coloured, with the shield divided vertically into red, white and black. In the past there have been other emblems on the flag. From 1972 to 1974 the emblem was a gold hawk facing the fly, similar to the one used by Syria since 1946. This was during the union with Syria and Libya known as the Federation of Arab Republics. Before 1972 the flag bore two green stars, to mark the United Arab Republic formed with Syria in 1958. The red, white and black flag was adopted in that year from the flag used by the National Liberation Movement, which overthrew the Egyptian monarchy in 1952, and has been the source of inspiration for the flags of several other Arab states. The present national emblem dates from 1958 and represents the Ayubite sultan, Saladin, and his victories over the crusaders. From 1958 to 1972 the shield also bore two green stars, but these do not appear in the current version, in which the title of the state is different as well. The falcon, used from 1972 to 1984 instead of the eagle, was the emblem of the Quraish tribe, the tribe to which the prophet Mohammed belonged. It appeared simultaneously on the flags of Egypt, Libya and Syria, but was abandoned by Libya in 1977 and was removed from the Syrian flag in 1980, although a form of it is still used as the Syrian emblem.

EQUATORIAL GUINEA
Republic
The flag has three horizontal stripes of green, white and red; based on the hoist there is a light blue isosceles triangle reaching to one-quarter of the flag's length. In the centre of the white stripe there is the state coat of arms which comprises a silver shield charged with a God tree in natural colours, ensigned with six golden six-pointed stars, representing the five islands and the mainland province of the country. The tree is taken from the municipal arms of Bata and it was under a God tree that a treaty was originally signed with the Spanish conquerors. Beneath the shield there is a white scroll with the motto UNIDAD, PAZ, JUSTICIA ("Unity, Peace, Justice"). Green stands for the agricultural wealth, red for the struggle for freedom, and white for peace and mutual understanding. The blue triangle represents the sea which links the mainland territory of the country and the islands. The

flag was introduced in 1968, but during the period 1976−9 under the regime of President Francisco Macías Nguema it bore a different central emblem.

ETHIOPIA
State with a provisional military government
The Ethiopian flag has three horizontal stripes of green, yellow and red. It was introduced in 1897, with the stripes in reversed order of colour, and was the first flag to bear the popular pan-African colours. These were later taken over by Ghana (in 1957) and then by a number of other African countries on achieving independence (namely Guinea, Cape Verde, Guinea-Bissau, Zaïre, São Tomé and Príncipe, Cameroon, Mali, Senegal, Togo, Dahomey (now Benin), Congo and Rwanda). It is probable that these colours were taken over from flags used in the Ethiopian army, or they may have been popular colours used in Ethiopian folk art. Acording to a long-standing official explanation, green symbolizes both the fertility of the land and hope, yellow stands for love of the fatherland, mineral wealth, peace and the church, and red represents strength and the blood shed for upholding freedom. Up to 1975 a crowned Ethiopian lion was depicted in the centre of the flag.

GABON
Republic
The flag of Gabon is a tricolour with horizontal stripes coloured green, yellow and blue, symbolizing the equator passing between green tropical forests and the blue waters of the sea; yellow also represents the sun. The flag has been used since 1958; before independence was proclaimed in 1960 the French tricolour appeared in the canton and the proportions of the stripes were 2 : 1 : 2.

THE GAMBIA
Republic within the British Commonwealth and, since 1982, member of the Confederation of Senegambia
The flag consists of three horizontal stripes coloured red, blue and green, separated by two narrow white stripes. The basic colours symbolize the sun, the River Gambia and the agriculture of the country; the white stripes stand for unity and peace. The widths of the individual stripes are in the proportions 6 : 1 : 4 : 1 : 6. The flag dates from 1965.

GHANA
Republic within the British Commonwealth
In 1957 Ghana was the first country of black Africa to achieve independence after World War II. Red, yellow and green stripes appeared on her flag, this being the original order of the colours of Ethiopia, the oldest independent African state. These colours have become the so-called pan-African colours which may, however, vary slightly in symbolism from country to country where they are used. On the Ghanaian

flag, red stands for independence and the blood of the heroes who fell during the struggle for freedom, yellow represents mineral wealth, especially gold, which gave the country its former name (the Gold Coast), and green is for the country's forests and fertile fields. A black five-pointed star symbolizes African unity and the black population. The flag was introduced in 1957; from 1964 to 1966 its central stripe was white, following the flag of the Convention People's Party which at that time was the only legal political party in the country.

GUINEA
Republic
The tricolour of Guinea comprises the popular pan-African colours in vertical stripes of red, yellow and green, which are also the colours of the Democratic Party of Guinea. Red stands for the blood shed for freedom and work and progress, green for agriculture and the extensive pasture-land in Futa Djalon, and yellow for gold and the sunshine which gives warmth equally to both the poor and the rich. The flag was introduced in 1958.

GUINEA-BISSAU
Republic
After the declaration of independence in 1973 and in accordance with a previously made decision, the 1961 flag of the African Party for the Independence of Guinea and Cape Verde (PAIGC) was accepted as the national flag. It has a red vertical stripe in the hoist, which occupies one third of the flag's length and is charged with a black five-pointed star drawn within an imaginary circle with a diameter of one-third of the flag's width. The remaining part of the flag is divided into two horizontal stripes — yellow over green. The black star symbolizes freedom, peace, the African people and their dignity; red denotes the fight for freedom, work and suffering during the times of oppression; yellow stands for the savannas of the north, harvest and the life-giving sun; and green stands for the forests of the south and the agricultural wealth of the country, together with the hope for a happy future.

IVORY COAST
Republic
The flag consists of three vertical stripes coloured orange, white and green. Orange stands for the savannas in the northern part of the country, green for the coastal forests of the south, and white represents the unity between the two parts of the state. Another explanation is that the colours symbolize respectively: the country's development, peace and purity, and the hope of the people. It has also been suggested that the colours denote the three words of the national motto: "Union, Discipline, Work". The colours are the same as those of the flag of

Ireland but they are in reverse order. The flag was created in 1959 and was inspired by the French tricolour.

KENYA
Republic within the British Commonwealth
The national flag is based on the 1952 tricolour of the Kenya African National Union (KANU), the political party which led the struggle for independence. The flag has horizontal stripes of black, red and green, and in 1963 two narrow white stripes were added (making the proportions 6 : 1 : 6 : 1 : 6). Black stands for the freedom-loving African population, red for their blood and the struggle for freedom, and green for the rich vegetation. The white stripes are symbols of peace and unity. In the centre of the flag there is a Masai war-shield in red, white and black, superimposed on two crossed spears. With these weapons, symbolizing the defence of freedom, the ancestors of today's population defended the country against their enemies. The flag dates from 1963.

LESOTHO
Kingdom within the British Commonwealth
The colours of the flag are taken from that of the ruling Lesotho National Party. In the hoist there are two narrow vertical stripes coloured green (symbol of the country) and red (faith and prayer). Each stripe occupies one-tenth of the flag's length. The remaining part of the flag is dark blue (representing the sky and rain), and in the centre there is a white silhouette of a Basuto straw hat, a traditional local product which stands for peace and the monarchy. The symbolism of the colours corresponds to the motto in the state coat of arms: "Peace, Rain, Prosperity". The flag was introduced in 1966.

LIBERIA
Republic
The flag of Liberia is based on the flag of the USA since it was through American initiative that this first black republic in Africa was established. Eleven horizontal stripes (six red and five white) recall the eleven signatories of the declaration of independence. The blue square canton, five stripes deep, represents the African continent, while the white five-pointed star stands for the shining light of Liberia. Red signifies valour, sincerity and endurance; blue is for freedom, justice and loyalty; and white represents purity, cleanliness and harmlessness. The flag in its present form dates from 1847 when independence was declared. From 1827 until 1847, when Liberia had the status of an American colony, the number of stripes (seven red and six white) and their colours were identical with those of the flag of the USA. The square canton was then seven stripes deep and contained a white couped cross.

LIBYA
Jamahiriya (state of the masses)
From 1971 to 1977 Libya, Egypt and Syria formed the Federation of Arab Republics and all flew the same flag. On 19 November 1977, however, the late President Sadat of Egypt opened talks with Israel and, in accordance with the decision of the Libyan General People's Parliament, Federation flags were burnt in protest against these negotiations. Immediately afterwards new provisional flags were hoisted on the buildings of Libyan diplomatic missions and other offices. These new flags are green, symbolizing Islam.

MADAGASCAR
Republic
The present Madagascar flag, derived from the flag of the Hova tribe, has a white vertical stripe in the hoist (occupying one-third of the flag's length) and two horizontal ones coloured red over green. White stands for purity of ideals, red for independence, and green for hope of a happy future. White and red were on the flags of the Hova kingdom of Madagascar in the 19th century, and green represents the inhabitants of the coasts. In addition, white is connected with the princely family of Volafotsi and red with the family of Volamena, both of which flourished in the 17th century. The flag was created in 1958 and was defined by the constitution one year later.

MALAWI
Republic within the British Commonwealth
A tricolour with horizontal stripes of black, red and green was adopted as the flag of the Malawi Congress Party in 1953. Black represents the African population; red stands for the blood of the martyrs for the freedom of Africa; and green is for the fertile land. On the declaration of independence in 1964 a red rising sun with thirty-one rays was added in the black stripe as a symbol of the dawning hope for freedom throughout the whole African continent. The flag has been used officially ever since.

MALI
Republic
Mali uses as her flag a tricolour with vertical stripes in the pan-African colours of green, yellow and red. These colours symbolize respectively hope and vegetation, the sun and mineral wealth, and gallantry and the revolutionary past of the people; they were also the colours of the African Democratic Rally, the political party which led the country to independence. The flag has been in use since 1961 and is derived from the 1959 flag of the Mali Federation (which united the then French Sudan (now Mali) and Senegal from 4 April 1959 until 20 August 1960). From 1959, however, a black stylized human figure, known as the "kanaga", had been included in the centre of the flag but this was

omitted after the dissolution of the Federation, following protests from Muslims, whose religion forbids the depiction of the human form. (See also the entry for Senegal on p. 130).

MAURITANIA
Republic
The green flag bears a yellow crescent with its horns pointing upwards and a yellow five-pointed star above it. Thus the strong influence of Islam in the country (the official name of which is the Islamic Republic of Mauritania) is expressed even in the design of the flag. Green also symbolizes prosperity and hope. The flag was introduced in 1959.

MAURITIUS
Independent member of the British Commonwealth
The flag consists of four horizontal stripes — red, blue, yellow and green — the colours being taken from the state coat of arms. Red represents the struggle for freedom and independence, and also the blood shed in this struggle; blue are the waves of the Indian Ocean washing the shores; yellow is the glow of freedom and new-found independence; and green stands for agricultural wealth and the colour of the vegetation throughout the whole year. The flag was introduced in 1968.

MOROCCO
Kingdom
The national flag comprises a green interlaced five-pointed star (the so-called "Solomon's seal") placed in the centre of a red field. Both these colours are traditionally Arabic. In Morocco red is interpreted as representing the freedom of the people, and green (the colour of Islam) stands for the hope for victory. The flag was introduced in 1915 when the previously plain red flag (used since the 17th century) had the star added to distinguish it from the red flags of other countries. Red is the colour of the reigning dynasty.

MOZAMBIQUE
People's republic
The flag of Mozambique is based on that used by the main nationalist movement, FRELIMO (the Mozambique Liberation Front), during the struggle for independence. It has three horizontal stripes of green, black and yellow, with a narrow white stripe above and below the black stripe. Based on the hoist is a red triangle, and on this is a simplified version of the national emblem, consisting of a yellow star surmounted by an open white book, surmounted in turn by a rifle crossed with a hoe. The colours represent the wealth of Mozambique's soil (green), the struggle for national liberation (red), the African continent (black), and the mineral wealth (yellow). White stands for justice and peace. The

book, hoe, and rifle represent education, the peasantry, and defence and vigilance, while the star stands for the building of a socialist economy and a socialist society. This version of the flag was introduced in April 1983 and replaced the one adopted on independence in June 1975, which had the same colours arranged in a different pattern, and a different version of the emblem in the canton.

NIGER
Republic
The flag of Niger has three horizontal stripes — orange, white and green — with an orange disc, symbolizing the sun, in the centre of the white stripe. This represents the readiness of the Nigérien people to sacrifice themselves in the struggle for the preservation of their rights. The orange stripe stands for the Sahara Desert, white for purity, innocence and ease of conscience after having done one's duty, and green for the grassy southern and western part of the country, and for brotherhood and hope. The flag is almost square (its proportions being 6 : 7) and dates from 1959.

NIGERIA
Federal republic within the British Commonwealth
The Nigerian flag consists of three vertical stripes — green, white and green. Green reflects the importance of agriculture, which forms the basis of the national economy, and white stands for peace and unity. The flag was officially adopted in 1960.

RWANDA
Republic
Rwanda's tricolour in the pan-African colours, with vertical stripes of red, yellow and green, was established in 1961. Later that year a black letter "R" was added in the centre of the yellow stripe to distinguish the flag of Rwanda from that of Guinea. This letter stands for Rwanda, revolution, referendum (from the slogan: "Rwanda created by revolution and confirmed by referendum"). Red is used in remembrance of the suffering and the blood of the Hutu people shed during the struggle for freedom; yellow signifies peace in the nation after a victorious revolution; and green symbolizes hope and trust in the future, and also the agricultural wealth of the country.

SÃO TOMÉ AND PRÍNCIPE
Republic
The national flag of this island republic is very similar to that of the Movement for the Liberation of São Tomé and Príncipe (MLSTP). It consists of three horizontal stripes of green, yellow and green (in the proportions 2 : 3 : 2) and a red triangle in the hoist, reaching to one-quarter of the flag's length. Two black five-pointed stars, representing the two

islands, are set in the central yellow stripe. Black also stands for the republic as part of black Africa, while red is for the martyrs' blood shed in the struggle for independence, green for the vegetation, and yellow for the cocoa plantations. The flag was introduced in 1975.

SENEGAL
Republic and, since 1982, member of the Confederation of Senegambia
The tricolour in the pan-African colours — with vertical stripes of green, yellow and red — is derived from the 1959 flag of the Mali Federation to which Senegal belonged, together with the then French Sudan (now Mali). It differs from the flags of the Federation and of Mali in having a green five-pointed star in its yellow stripe; this star symbolizes hope and African unity, and is a substitute for the emblem (now omitted) on the flag of Mali. The colours of the flag represent the three principles (unity, democracy and equality) adopted at the time of the anti-colonial struggle. The flag dates from 1960.

SENEGAMBIA
Confederation of Senegal and The Gambia
Both member countries are still using their individual flags and arms, no common state symbols having yet been created.

SEYCHELLES
Republic within the British Commonwealth
The upper part of the flag is red, the lower one green, separated by a wavy white stripe. The proportions of these three fields at the edge of the flag are 3 : 1 : 2. Red symbolizes progress and revolution, and also sweat and toil which used to be the lot of the people of the Seychelles and which will now help in building a proud and worthy state. The white stripe represents the waters of the Indian Ocean surrounding the islands, and its resources. Green stands for the islands' vegetation. The flag was introduced after the coup d'état in 1977 (replacing the first flag when the Seychelles gained independence in 1976) and is derived from the flag of the Seychelles People's United Party which has, in addition, a yellow rising sun of freedom.

SIERRA LEONE
Republic within the British Commonwealth
The flag consists of three horizontal stripes of green, white and cobalt blue. Green stands for agriculture, natural resources and the country's mountains; white is for peace, justice and unity; and blue represents the waters of the Atlantic Ocean washing the beaches, and the hope that the harbour of the capital, Freetown, can contribute to world peace through the development of commerce passing through it. The flag was introduced at the declaration of independence in 1961.

SOMALIA
Republic

The visually well-balanced flag of this former trust territory of the United Nations comprises a large white five-pointed star in the centre of a blue field, these colours being taken from the United Nations flag. Blue stands for the bright sky, the white star for African freedom, its five points representing the five regions in which the Somali people lived at the time when the flag was created: Italian Somaliland, British Somaliland (both of which now form Somalia), French Somaliland (now Djibouti), Kenya and Ethiopia. The flag originally flew in Italian Somaliland, where it was officially recognized in 1954.

SOUTH AFRICA
Republic

The South African flag — with its horizontal stripes of orange, white and blue — is a true representation of the original Dutch flag which was hoisted here by the Dutch in 1652 at the beginning of the colonization of this territory. In the white stripe there is a small British flag, representing the Cape Province and Natal and simultaneously commemorating the beginning of the British occupation of southern Africa in 1795. Beside the Union Flag are the flags of the Orange Free State and the Transvaal; both these flags belonged to the Boer republics subdued by the British in the Boer War (1899 — 1902), who turned them into two new provinces. (The union of all four provinces in 1910 brought the Union of South Africa into being.) The Orange Free State flag of 1856 has three orange stripes on a white field, and the Dutch flag in the canton; this design was granted to the Orange Free State by King William III of the Netherlands as a reminder of the Dutch origin of its inhabitants. The four-coloured flag of the Transvaal (the "Vierkleur") of 1857 was created by the addition of a green vertical stripe (a symbol of the "Young Netherlands") in the hoist of the Dutch tricolour. The South African flag was officially introduced in 1928 as a reminder of the first organized colonization of the Cape Colony by the Dutch. The flags of the United Kingdom and the Boer republics are meant to symbolize appeasement and the co-existence of the English and Boer inhabitants in one state. The South African flag is also used in Namibia and the Prince Edward Islands.

SUDAN
Republic

The so-called "Arab Liberation" colours in horizontal stripes of red, white and black form the basis of the Sudanese flag, and in the hoist there is a green isosceles triangle reaching to one-third of the flag's length. According to one interpretation, green is the colour of the historical Arab dynasty of the Fatimids, of Islam and of prosperity; red stands for revolution, progress, socialism and the nation's martyrs;

white is for light, peace, optimism and for the white flag of the 1924 revolution; and black refers both to the southern part of the country being in black Africa and to the fact that Sudan means "black" in Arabic. In addition, black was the chief colour of the Mahdi, who unified Sudan in the last century. The flag was introduced in 1970.

SWAZILAND
Kingdom within the British Commonwealth
The flag has five horizontal stripes coloured blue, yellow, crimson, yellow and blue (the proportions being 3 : 1 : 8 : 1 : 3). In the centre of the broad crimson stripe there is a horizontally placed war shield of the historical Emasotsha regiment; placed vertically, it also forms part of the state coat of arms. The shield is black and white and made of oxhide, and on it there is a blue decorative tuft of feathers. Behind the shield there are two spears with their points to the right and a Zulu fighting stick with two more blue tufts attached to its ends. These tufts, which are called "tinjobo",are royal attributes. Crimson recalls the battles of the Swazis in the past, while yellow stands for mineral wealth and blue for peace. The draft of this flag was prepared in 1954 and was inspired by the colours of the Swazi Pioneer Corps of 1941, which were given to its commander by the Swazi king as a reminder of the military traditions of the Swazis. The flag has been officially used since 1967.

TANZANIA
Republic within the British Commonwealth
The flag is divided into two triangles by a broad black stripe running diagonally from the lower hoist to the upper fly, bordered by two narrow yellow stripes; the triangle in the hoist is green and the other is blue. Green symbolizes the fertile land; blue stands for the sea (according to some interpretations, for Zanzibar); black is for the ethnic majority of Tanzania; and yellow represents her mineral wealth. In addition, the position of the black stripe and the colour of its borders suggest the continuing development of the black population amid prosperity. The flag was created in 1964 by combining the features of the flags of Tanganyika and Zanzibar when the two countries joined together to form a union. The Tanganyikan flag had three horizontal stripes — green, black and green — which were the colours of the Tanganyika African National Union (TANU) and which were separated from each other by narrow yellow stripes; the flag of Zanzibar had horizontal stripes of blue, black and green, with a narrow white stripe in the hoist. Both these flags are still used locally.

TOGO
Republic
The flag, in the well-known pan-African colours, has three green horizontal stripes alternating with two yellow stripes and a red square

canton charged with a white five-pointed star which symbolizes unity and shines on the path of progress. Green stands for agriculture and agricultural wealth; yellow represents mining, faith and the people's strength; red is for humanity, patriotism, fidelity and love of the fatherland; and white denotes purity. The flag was introduced in 1960.

TUNISIA
Republic
Tunisia once belonged to the Ottoman Empire and this is reflected in the flag which is red with a white disc in the middle, representing the sun and containing a red Osmanli (Turkish) crescent and a five-pointed star — the two ancient symbols of Islam. The shape of the waxing moon (from the point of view of an Arab observer of the flag) brings luck. Although red had been the colour of the second caliph, Omar I, it was the Ottoman Empire which elevated it to the state colour. In spite of this, in some Arab countries red became a symbol of resistance against Turkish supremacy. The flag dates from 1835, and it became the national flag on the declaration of independence of Tunisia in 1956.

UGANDA
Republic within the British Commonwealth
The flag consists of six horizontal stripes — black, yellow, red, black, yellow and red. In the centre of the flag is an old badge of Uganda, the crested crane on a white disc. Black, yellow and red were colours of the political party known as the Uganda People's Congress. Black symbolizes Africa and the black population of the country; yellow is the colour of the life-giving sun; and red stands for fraternity between all people. The flag dates from 1962.

ZAIRE
Republic
The flag of light green has a yellow disc in its centre on which a dark brown human arm holding a brown torch with red flames is depicted. Green is the colour of the Popular Movement of the Revolution (MPR) and also signifies peace, hope and faith; yellow represents the country's immense mineral wealth; and red stands for the blood of the martyrs for freedom. The central position of the disc symbolizes unity and the flaming torch stands for revolution. The flag was introduced in 1971 following the change of name from the Democratic Republic of the Congo (previously Belgian Congo) so that it would be completely different from that of the People's Republic of the Congo (a former French colony).

ZAMBIA
Republic within the British Commonwealth
The flag of Zambia is green. Its bottom fly bears a tricolour of vertical stripes coloured red, black and orange, above which is an orange

eagle from the state coat of arms, with spread wings. The eagle, which had previously appeared in the arms of Northern Rhodesia (Zambia's former name) is the symbol of the Zambian desire for freedom and the people's ability to solve the country's problems. Green represents the natural wealth of the country in her forests and fields; red signifies the struggle for freedom; black stands for the people of Zambia; and orange is for her mineral wealth, especially copper. These are also the colours of the ruling United National Independence Party (UNIP). The flag was introduced in 1964.

ZIMBABWE
Republic within the British Commonwealth
The flag of Zimbabwe has seven horizontal stripes coloured green, yellow, red, black, red, yellow and green; a white isosceles triangle, based on the hoist, reaches to one-third of the flag's length and is separated from the horizontal stripes by a narrow black border. The triangle contains a red five-pointed star over which is placed the Zimbabwe bird in yellow (representing gold); this bird overlaps the star into the triangular field. Green signifies the land and its agricultural resources; yellow is for the country's wealth; red stands for the blood shed in the struggle for freedom; and black represents the ethnic majority of the population. These colours were taken from the flag of the dominant Zimbabwe African National Union (ZANU), to which white was added to symbolize pacification between the white and black sections of the population. The red five-pointed star is an expression of the internationalist outlook of the people, and the depiction of the legendary bird from the ruins of Zimbabwe, which is the country's symbol, recalls her glorious past. The flag was introduced at the time of Zimbabwe's declaration of independence in 1980, and followed the flags of Zimbabwe-Rhodesia (1979), Rhodesia (1968), Southern Rhodesia (1964), and Rhodesia and Nyasaland (1963).

Dependent Territories

AZORES
Autonomous part of Portugal
The regional flag of the Azores is divided vertically into two unequal stripes of dark blue and white (with the proportions 2:3). Over the dividing line there is a golden goshawk surmounted by nine golden five-pointed stars arranged in an arc. The Portuguese state coat of arms, which is a sign of sovereignty, appears in the upper hoist. The goshawk (açor) is the symbol of the Azores, which are named after the bird, and the stars represent the nine main islands. The blue-and-white flag is derived from the former royal Portuguese flag, and it is also linked with the flag of the Azores Liberation Front which favoured autonomy. The flag was introduced in 1979.

CANARY ISLANDS
Autonomous region of Spain
The flag consists of three vertical stripes of white, blue and yellow. These are colours of the National Party of the Canary Islands which was founded early in the 20th century in Cuba. White stands for the snow-covered summit of the Pico de Teide volcano, blue for the sea, and yellow for the wealth created by the labour of the inhabitants.

MADEIRA
Autonomous part of Portugal
The regional flag of Madeira consists of three vertical stripes of blue, yellow and blue. The white-and-red cross of the Knights of the Order of Christ, the local symbol of separatism, is placed in the centre of the yellow stripe. Blue and yellow are traditional local colours: blue symbolizes the Atlantic Ocean surrounding the island and also represents beauty, brightness and peace; yellow stands for the agreeable climate, together with wealth, strength, faith and unity. The flag was introduced in 1978.

MAYOTTE
French overseas territory with special status
The French flag is used.

NAMIBIA
Territory unlawfully occupied by South Africa; previously League of Nations mandated territory
The South African flag is used.

RÉUNION
French overseas department
The French flag is used.

ST HELENA AND DEPENDENCIES
British dependent territory
The British Blue Ensign with the local badge in the fly is used. This consists of an ornamental shield displaying a three-masted ship of the East India Company sailing between two rocky outcrops, and flying the red cross of St George, all in natural colours.

SPANISH NORTH AFRICA
Spanish territory (comprising the cities of Ceuta and Melilla, with the small islands of Peñón de Alhucemas, Peñón de Vélez de la Gomera, and Chafarinas off the Moroccan coast)
The Spanish state flag is used. In addition, Ceuta and Melilla fly their own city flags beside the Spanish flag.

NORTH AND CENTRAL AMERICA

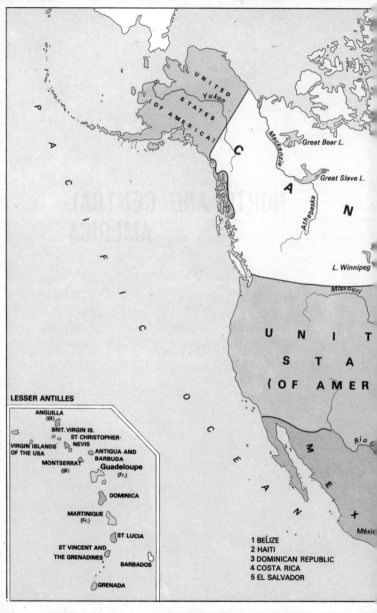

NORTH AND CENTRAL AMERICA

UNITED STATES (OF AMERICA)

Yukon

C A N A D A

Great Bear L.

Great Slave L.

Mackenzie

Athabaska

L. Winnipeg

Missouri

U N I T

S T A

(OF AMER

M E X

Rio G

México

PACIFIC OCEAN

LESSER ANTILLES

ANGUILLA (UK)

BRIT. VIRGIN IS.

ST CHRISTOPHER-NEVIS

VIRGIN ISLANDS OF THE USA

ANTIGUA AND BARBUDA

MONTSERRAT (UK)

Guadeloupe (Fr.)

DOMINICA

MARTINIQUE (Fr.)

ST LUCIA

ST VINCENT AND THE GRENADINES

BARBADOS

GRENADA

1 BELIZE
2 HAITI
3 DOMINICAN REPUBLIC
4 COSTA RICA
5 EL SALVADOR

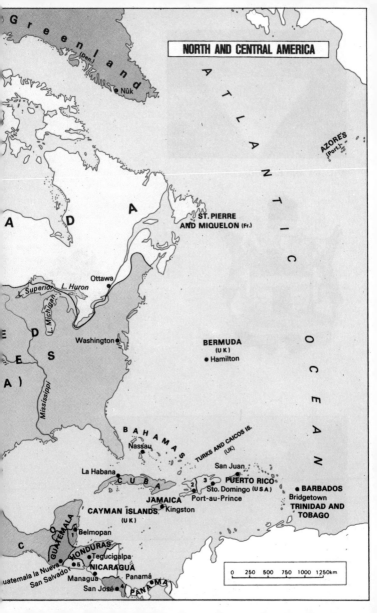

NORTH AND CENTRAL AMERICA

ANTIGUA AND BARBUDA (2:3)

BAHAMAS (1:2)

BARBADOS (2:3)

BELIZE (2:3)

141

CANADA(1:2)

COSTA RICA(3:5)

CUBA (1:2)

DOMINICA (1:2)

DOMINICAN REPUBLIC (2:3)

EL SALVADOR (3:5)

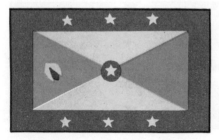

GRENADA (3:5)

144

GUATEMALA(5:8)

HAITI(1:2)

145

HONDURAS(1:2)

JAMAICA(1:2)

MEXICO (4:7)

NICARAGUA (3:5)

PANAMA (2:3)

ST CHRISTOPHER-NEVIS (2:3)

ST LUCIA (1:2)

ST VINCENT AND THE GRENADINES (4:7)

UNITED STATES OF AMERICA (10:19)

Anguilla (1:2)

Bermuda (1:2)

British Virgin Islands (1:2)

Cayman Islands (1:2)

Martinique (2:3)

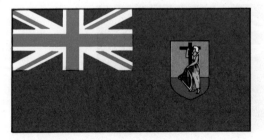

Montserrat (1:2)

151

Puerto Rico (2:3)

St Pierre and Miquelon (2:3)

Turks and Caicos Islands (1:2)

Virgin Islands of the USA (2:3)

ANTIGUA AND BARBUDA
Independent state within the British Commonwealth
The flag is red bearing a large isosceles triangle, the base of which is at the upper edge of the flag and the apex in the middle of the lower edge. The triangle is divided into three horizontal sections of black, blue and white (the proportions being 3 : 2 : 3). The black stripe bears a yellow rising sun with nine rays symbolizing the entry into a new era of the state's development. The "V" shape suggests victory over colonialism. The red colour symbolizes the creative dynamism of the people; black suggests the African origin of the majority of the inhabitants; and blue stands for hope. Yellow, blue and white together stand for the sun, the sea and the sandy beaches of the islands, i.e. their main tourist attractions. The flag was introduced in 1967 and remained unchanged on the declaration of independence in 1981.

THE BAHAMAS
Independent state within the British Commonwealth
The flag of the Bahamas consists of three horizontal stripes — blue, golden yellow and blue — with a black equilateral triangle based on the hoist. This triangle symbolizes the determination of the Bahamian people to develop and to dominate the rich natural resources of both land and sea. Yellow represents the islands' coasts and the sun, and blue is for the sea. Black stands for the strength and power of the united Bahamian nation. The flag was introduced in 1973.

BARBADOS
Independent state within the British Commonwealth
The flag consists of three vertical stripes, golden yellow in the middle (symbolizing the sand of the island's beaches) between two blue ones (representing the sea and sky surrounding the island). In the centre there is a black trident of the sea god Neptune (suggesting the link between the islanders' life and the sea), the three points of which symbolize the principles of democratic government — from the people, with the people, and for the people. The trident was part of the island's badge during the colonial period, but after the declaration of independence the shaft was removed to stress that Barbados had made a clean break with her past. The flag was adopted in 1966.

BELIZE
Independent state within the British Commonwealth
The flag is dark blue with a narrow red stripe at both the upper and lower edges (each stripe taking up one-tenth of the flag's width). In the centre there is a large white circular field charged with the state coat of arms within a wreath of fifty green laurel leaves. The shield

in the arms is divided into three sections, each bearing an illustration. In the upper left section a heavy hammer is crossed over a paddle. In the upper right section a two-handed saw is crossed over an axe; this represents tree-felling and the transportation of timber, especially of mahogany (a mahogany tree appears in the crest), which was formerly the basis of the country's economy. In the bottom section the transportation of timber to Europe is recalled by a three-masted sailing ship. The supporters are a Mestizo (with an axe) and a Creole (with a paddle). The scroll bears the motto SUB UMBRA FLOREO ("I flourish in the shade"). The number of leaves in the laurel wreath symbolizes the year 1950 when the movement for the liberation of the country from British rule became active. The flag has been used since the declaration of independence in 1981, and is derived from the flag of the ruling People's United Party, which had been used semi-officially and more generally since 1965. At the request of the opposition party, the United Democratic Party, they were represented by the addition of the two red stripes to the flag.

CANADA
Independent state within the British Commonwealth
The Canadian flag consists of three vertical stripes of red, white and red, their proportions being 1 : 2 : 1; in the middle of the white stripe there is a stylized red maple leaf which has been used as Canada's national symbol for the past century or more. The red stripes on both sides of the maple leaf are symbolical of Canada's position between the two oceans (the original draft stated that the stripes were to be blue), in accordance with the motto in the state coat of arms, which means "From sea to sea". Red and white have been the official Canadian colours since 1921 when red was incorporated in the new coat of arms to symbolize the blood of the Canadians who fell in World War I and white to represent the snow of the Canadian north. The flag was introduced in 1965 when it replaced the previously used Red Ensign with the shield from the Canadian arms in the fly.

COSTA RICA
Republic
The flag consists of five horizontal stripes — blue, white, red, white and blue (the proportions being 1 : 1 : 2 : 1 : 1) — and towards the hoist of the red stripe a white oval bears the state coat of arms of 1848. In later years the arms have been repeatedly amended, most recently in 1964; they comprise a gold-rimmed shield depicting three brown Costa Rican volcanoes (Barba, Irazú and Poás) washed by the Caribbean Sea and the Pacific Ocean, on the waves of which there are two sailing ships. A golden sun of freedom rises on the horizon and in the blue sky above the mountains there are seven five-pointed stars which represent the seven provinces of Costa Rica. Until 1964 there were only five stars,

which represented the five original member countries of the former United Provinces of Central America (1823 – 39) — Costa Rica, Honduras, Guatemala, Nicaragua and El Salvador. Above the stars there is a white scroll with the words REPUBLICA DE COSTA RICA in blue letters, and above the shield there is a light-blue scroll with the words AMERICA CENTRAL in dark-blue letters. Originally the colours of the flag were blue and white as in the flags of all the countries of the federation, but in 1848 a red stripe was added and this gave the flag the colours of the French tricolour in honour of the French Revolution. These colours symbolize the revolutionary motto "Liberty, Equality, Fraternity".

CUBA
Socialist republic
The Cuban flag has five horizontal stripes (three blue and two white) and a red equilateral triangle charged with a white five-pointed star in the hoist. The blue stripes represent the three departments into which the island was divided at the time of liberation; the white stripes stand for purity and the high ideals of the Cubans fighting for independence, and the red triangle recalls the three ideals of the revolution — freedom, equality and fraternity. Red denotes the blood shed for independence. The white star is the star of freedom. The flag, called "La Estrella Solitaria" ("The Lone Star"), was created in 1849 in the USA and was influenced by the American flag. The Cuban flag was officially adopted when the country was liberated in 1902, but had been hoisted for the first time on Cuban soil by General Narciso López when he landed in 1850 at Cárdenas in an attempt to liberate the island.

DOMINICA
Republic within the British Commonwealth
The flag is dark green and bears a cross composed of three stripes — yellow, black and white; in the centre there is a red disc with a diameter equal to two-thirds of the flag's width. The disc is charged with ten green five-pointed stars which are edged with yellow and arranged in a circle around a "sisserou"(Imperial Parrot), perched on a brown twig. This parrot, which lives only in Dominica, is depicted in its proper colours — predominantly green, but with blue on the head, the back and the breast. Red appears under its wings, and the legs and beak are yellow; the eye is white with a black pupil. This is the national bird of the island and symbolizes "flight toward greater heights and fulfilment of aspirations". Red stands for the socialist programme of development adopted by Dominica, and the number of stars corresponds to the ten administrative divisions (parishes). The cross denotes the religious feeling of the people, while its three stripes symbolize, according to the official description, the Holy Trinity. Yellow is for the sun, the citrus fruits and bananas, and also for the indigenous Carib Indians of Dominica; black represents the soil and the African origin of the majority of the inhabitants;

and white stands for the clear waters of the island and the purity of the nation's aspirations. Green denotes the forests and rich vegetation of the island. The flag was introduced on the declaration of independence of Dominica in 1978 and replaced the former flag which comprised the British Blue Ensign with the Dominican coat of arms in the fly. Until the end of 1981 the order of the stripes in the cross was yellow, white and then black, while the parrot had a slightly different attitude, and the ten stars were lime-green in colour.

DOMINICAN REPUBLIC
Republic
The flag is divided by a white cross into four quarters, the first and the fourth being blue and the second and third red. In the centre of the cross in the state flag there is the state coat of arms of 1844. Its shield bears a repetition of the flag's pattern with the addition of four crossed flags and two crossed spears, and in the middle there is a Bible open at the Gospel of St John (Chapter One), ensigned with a golden cross which symbolizes liberation from slavery. The shield is framed by two green branches, one of laurel and the other of palm, bound together with a ribbon in the national colours. A red scroll under the shield is inscribed REPUBLICA DOMINICANA, and a blue scroll above bears the national motto: DIOS, PATRIA, LIBERTAD (which means "God, father-land, liberty"). The cross on the flag symbolizes the sacrifices of the people, together with their faith and strength; blue stands for freedom gained, and red for the blood and fire of the struggle for freedom. The original design of this flag, called "La Trinitaria" (after a movement for secession from Haiti, which had the same name), dates from 1839 but the flag was not used until after the declaration of independence in 1844. The blue and red are taken from the then flag of Haiti, and the white cross was added as a symbol of faith and sacrifice. It was only later that the red and blue quarters in the fly were counterchanged for aesthetic reasons.

EL SALVADOR
Republic
The flag is composed of three horizontal stripes of blue, white and blue; these are the colours of the former United Provinces of Central America (1823 – 39), its original member states being El Salvador, Honduras, Guatemala, Costa Rica and Nicaragua. The blue stripes symbolize the waters of the Caribbean Sea and the Pacific Ocean which wash the coasts of these countries, and white is the colour of peace and understanding. The state coat of arms of El Salvador is placed in the centre of the state flag, and is based on that of the federation. The arms depict a gold-rimmed triangle (its sides representing equality, truth and law) in which five green volcanoes, symbolizing the individual member states of the federation, rise from the dividing line between two

oceans. Above them there are the red Phrygian cap of freedom raised on top of a pole, the rising sun, and the rainbow of peace. In the rays of the sun there is a date — 15 DE SEPTIEMBRE DE 1821 (the date of liberation from Spanish rule) — arranged in a semicircle. Behind the triangle there are five federation flags and beneath it there is a white scroll with the motto DIOS, UNION, LIBERTAD (which means "God, union, liberty"). The whole is framed by a laurel wreath bound at the bottom with a blue ribbon, the fourteen clusters of leaves corresponding to the number of El Salvador's departments. On the flag these arms are surrounded by the following in gold letters: REPUBLICA DE EL SALVADOR EN LA AMERICA CENTRAL. This flag with the arms has been in use since 1912 but it was also used without the arms during the period 1823—65. The most recent law regulating the coat of arms was issued in 1972.

GRENADA
Independent state within the British Commonwealth
The flag of Grenada has a broad red border bearing three yellow five-pointed stars at the upper and lower edges. The inner rectangular field is divided diagonally into four triangles, the left and right ones being green and the upper and lower ones being yellow. The left-hand triangle bears a brown nutmeg in a yellow shell. In the centre of the flag there is a red disc charged with yet another yellow star. Red denotes the fervour, courage and vitality of the Grenadian people, together with their "burning aspiration to be free"; the red border affirms the determination of the inhabitants to maintain "harmony and unity of spirit". Yellow represents "wisdom, the sun which shines on the island, and the warmth and friendliness of the people". Green stands for fertility, the abundant vegetation and agriculture. The stars denote hope, the aspirations and the ideals with which the Grenadian nation was born, while their number corresponds to the seven administrative divisions of the country (including the Grenadines). Nutmeg is a traditional agricultural product of Grenada (which accounts for nearly one-quarter of the total world production of nutmeg) and recalls the former name of the island — the Isle of Spice. The flag was introduced on the declaration of independence of Grenada in 1974.

GUATEMALA
Republic
The state flag of Guatemala consists of three vertical stripes of blue, white and blue, and bears in the centre the state coat of arms of 1871 (which follows the pattern of 1843). It features the quetzal — Guatemala's national bird, symbolizing freedom (it is reputed not to be able to live in captivity) — in natural colours. The quetzal perches on a parchment with the text LIBERTAD 15 DE SEPTIEMBRE DE 1821, the date of liberation from the Spaniards and the proclamation of independence. The back-

ground is formed by crossed rifles with fixed bayonets and crossed sabres, framed by a laurel wreath. The colours of the flag's stripes are those of the United Provinces of Central America (1823 – 39) to which Guatemala belonged together with Honduras, Costa Rica, Nicaragua and El Salvador as the other original members, but, unlike the flags of these four countries, the stripes are arranged vertically. They nevertheless symbolize the position of the federation between the Caribbean Sea and the Pacific Ocean. Blue also signifies the independence of the country, and white stands for peace. The flag with the present arms has been in use since 1871 and was finally approved, with alterations to the coat of arms, in 1968.

HAITI
Republic
The state flag consists of two vertical stripes of black and red and bears in the centre a white rectangle featuring the 1806 state coat of arms of Haiti, as amended in 1964 when the cap of liberty was deleted and the flag colours changed. The arms depict a green lawn and a military drum behind which there are two crossed axes and a palm tree in proper colours. These are flanked by two cannon, flags, anchors and guns with fixed bayonets. Underneath there is a white scroll with the motto L'UNION FAIT LA FORCE (which means "Union gives strength") in black letters. The whole recalls the country's struggle for freedom early in the 19th century. Black stands for the black inhabitants and their African heritage, and red is for the struggle for independence. In the past red also represented the mulattos. Since 1798 the French tricolour had flown in the island but in 1804 the leader of the insurgents against the French, Jean-Jacques Dessalines, removed the white stripe which represented friendship with the French; the Haitians also regarded this colour as a symbol of white slavery. When Dessalines became emperor in 1804, he replaced the blue stripe with a black one. After Dessalines' assassination President Alexandre Sabès Pétion renewed the blue and red colours in the southern part of the country, and these were used either in horizontal or vertical stripes. After 1806, however, the horizontal arrangement prevailed and when President Jean-Paul Boyer came to power in 1818 a flag of blue over red was adopted. In 1844 the coat of arms set in a white rectangle was added but in 1964 the second pattern of the flag was restored, i.e. vertical stripes of black and red.

HONDURAS
Republic
The flag is composed of three horizontal stripes – blue, white and blue – and five blue five-pointed stars (2 + 1 + 2) are borne in the centre of the white stripe. Blue represents the waters of the Pacific Ocean and the Caribbean Sea between which the country lies, and white stands for the unity of the country.The arrangement of the stripes is the same

as that in the flag of the United Provinces of Central America (1823 – 39) which originally comprised Honduras, Guatemala, El Salvador, Nicaragua and Costa Rica. These five countries are also represented by the five stars on the flag which symbolize the hope that these states will eventually reunite. The flag has been in use since 1866 and was officially confirmed in 1949.

JAMAICA
Independent state within the British Commonwealth
The flag is divided by a golden yellow saltire into four triangles, the upper and lower ones being green and those in the hoist and fly being black. Yellow symbolizes the beauty of sunlight and the mineral wealth of the island, and green stands for hope and agriculture. Black represents the heavy burden of subjugation which the people had to carry and the current difficulties which they have to face. The flag was introduced in 1962.

MEXICO
Federal republic
The Mexican tricolour has vertical stripes coloured green, white and red, and bears in the centre the state coat of arms of 1823 as amended in 1968. The arms consist of a brown eagle standing on top of a nopal cactus, which grows from an island in a lake, and holding in its beak a green snake; underneath there are two sprigs, one of oak and the other of laurel, forming a semicircle and bound with a ribbon in the national colours. These arms illustrate an old Aztec legend according to which the wandering Indian people had to settle on an island in the middle of a lake where they would see such a scene; this place was found in Lake Texcoco, and Tenochtitlán, now Mexico City, was founded there in about 1325. Green stands for independence, white for the purity of religion, and red for the equality of Spanish, Indian and Mestizo blood. The flag was introduced in 1821, at first with the stripes in a different order and arranged diagonally. Since 1823 it has had the present arrangement of the stripes and has borne the coat of arms, although the arms have often undergone changes in detail. The present shape and design of the flag date from 1968.

NICARAGUA
Republic
The state flag of Nicaragua consists of three horizontal stripes of blue, white and blue and bears the 1908 state coat of arms in the centre. The central part of the arms is a triangle (its sides symbolizing equality, truth and law) in which five green volcanoes rise up on a strip of land between two oceans. The volcanoes represent Nicaragua, Honduras, Guatemala, Costa Rica and El Salvador, which were the five original members of the United Provinces of Central America (1823 – 39). Floating

above them and beneath a rainbow of peace there is the Phrygian cap of liberty within a halo of white rays. Around the triangle there is a yellow circular inscription which reads: REPUBLICA DE NICARAGUA — AMERICA CENTRAL. The colours were taken from the United Provinces flag of 1823, and the "volcano" coat of arms is very similar to that used by this federation in the same year. The symbolism of the flag's colours is made explicit by the illustration in the arms: the blue stripes represent the waters of the Caribbean Sea and the Pacific Ocean which wash the coasts of the five adjoining countries. Blue also stands for justice and fidelity, and white is for purity and honesty. The flag has been used since 1908, and previously from 1823 to 1854. It was finally approved in 1971.

PANAMA
Republic
The flag has four quarters. The first is white with a blue five-pointed star, the second red, the third blue, and the fourth white with a red five-pointed star. White stands for peace and freedom; red and blue represent the chief political parties of the country (the Liberals and the Conservatives); and the stars signify fidelity and strength (according to another interpretation they represent the cities of Panamá and Colón which are at either end of the Panama Canal). The orderly division of the colours is intended to suggest alternation of these parties in governing the country. Blue is also said to stand for the waters of the Caribbean Sea and the Pacific Ocean while red is the symbol of the blood which the patriots shed for freedom. According to the flag's designer the blue star signifies civic virtues and the red star authority and law which protect them. The flag was created in 1903 (officially confirmed in 1904) and clearly recalls the flag of the USA which influenced the secession of Panama from Colombia.

ST CHRISTOPHER-NEVIS
Independent state within the British Commonwealth
A new flag was adopted for St Christopher-Nevis (the former is known locally as St Kitts) when the islands became independent on 19 September 1983. This flag is divided diagonally by a black band edged in yellow and bearing two white stars whose upper points are directed towards the top left-hand side of the flag. The triangle based on the hoist is green and the other is red. This flag replaced the one flown in the islands since February 1967, which was divided vertically into green, yellow and blue bands with a black palm tree with three roots in the centre. The symbolism of the new flag is that the green stands for the fertile land, yellow for the ever-present sunshine, black for the heritage of the people, red for the struggle for emancipation, and the two stars represent hope and liberty.

ST LUCIA
Independent state within the British Commonwealth
The flag is blue with an upright black isosceles triangle which has a white stripe along the upper two sides. Overlying this triangle, on the same base line, there is a smaller yellow isosceles triangle. Blue symbolizes the waters of the Caribbean Sea and the Atlantic Ocean, and yellow represents the island's beaches and sunshine. Black and white stand for the two predominant races among the inhabitants who live and work together. The black triangle also recalls the two summits of the famous Piton volcano (Gros Piton and Petit Piton), a tourist attraction which is both a symbol of the island and an important landmark for ships sailing near by. The flag dates from 1967, when its proportions were 5 : 8 and the yellow triangle was not so high. The present pattern (with the proportions of 1 : 2) dates from 1979, when independence was proclaimed.

ST VINCENT AND THE GRENADINES
Independent state within the British Commonwealth
The flag consists of three vertical stripes of blue, yellow and green (the proportions being 10 : 11 : 10) separated from each other by narrow bands of white. In the middle of the yellow stripe there is a green breadfruit leaf surmounted by the coat of arms of St Vincent, which comprises a white shield with a green base, two priestesses dressed in blue and, between them, an altar with a fire on top. The kneeling woman holds a golden offering bowl, while the standing one holds an olive branch. Above the shield there is the crest: a sprig of cotton on a white and green torse. Beneath the shield there is a white scroll with the motto PAX ET JUSTITIA (meaning "Peace and Justice") which is personified by the two women on the shield. Blue stands for the sky and the sea, yellow for tropical sunshine, green for the vegetation and white for purity. The flag was introduced in 1979, the previous flag being the British Blue Ensign with a circular badge in the fly.

UNITED STATES OF AMERICA
Federal Republic
The current American flag consists of thirteen horizontal stripes — seven red alternating with six white — with a blue canton equal in width to seven stripes; the canton is charged with fifty white five-pointed stars arranged in nine rows (six stars alternating with five). The stripes represent the thirteen original founder-states of the North American Union, and the stars stand for the present total of member states. These criteria have been in force since 1818 but the first flag of the United States, the famous Stars and Stripes, dates from 1777, and the current pattern (dating from 1960) is the twenty-seventh version. According to legend, it was George Washington himself who interpreted the individual elements of the flag in this way: the stars were taken from the sky, the red from the British colours, and the white stripes signified the

secession from the home country. The first American flag with thirteen stripes, called the "Great Union Flag", "Congress Flag" or "Continental Colours" — which had been created in the autumn of 1775 — became the national flag of the USA in 1776; at that time, however, the British Union Flag occupied the canton. The Congress Flag was indeed strikingly similar to the flag of the British East India Company (well known in American waters) but the former was possibly derived from the British Red Ensign by the addition of six white stripes. The American flag served as the model for the flags of Puerto Rico, Cuba, Liberia, Malaysia, Chile and Uruguay. It is flown in all the American dependencies, and also, together with the flag of the United Nations and the flag of Micronesia, in those islands.

Dependent Territories

ANGUILLA
British dependent territory
The flag of Anguilla consists of two horizontal stripes, white over greenish blue in the proportions 8 : 3. Three orange dolphins interlocked in a circle, symbolizing the strength and endurance of the islanders, are depicted in the middle of the white field. White denotes devotion to peace, while blue stands for youth, hope, prosperity and the surrounding sea. The flag was introduced in 1967 when Anguilla made an attempt to gain independence, and it is still currently used although according to the statute of 1980 the official flag of the island is the British Union Flag.

BERMUDA
British dependent territory
In Bermuda the British merchant flag (the Red Ensign) with the Bermuda badge of 1910 in the fly is used, and this is the only case of the Red Ensign being used as a distinctive flag in any British dependency. This is probably a reminder of the fact that the first settlers came in British ships flying this particular flag. The shield of the badge features a seated red lion supporting another shield with an illustration of the "Sea Venture" sinking by a reef called to this day the Sea Venture Flat. With Admiral

George Somers on board, this ship foundered here in 1609, and the islands bore his name for a short time afterwards. The survivors were the first, even if only temporary, settlers of Bermuda.

Bermuda

British Virgin Islands

BRITISH VIRGIN ISLANDS
British dependent territory
The British Blue Ensign with the islands' badge of 1960 is used. The badge is placed in the fly and consists of a green shield bearing the figure of a virgin in white robes carrying an ancient golden oil lamp, flanked by eleven similar lamps. The motto under the shield says VIGILATE (which means "Be watchful").

CAYMAN ISLANDS
British dependent territory
The British Blue Ensign with the islands' badge of 1958 is used, the badge being placed on a white disc in the fly. The shield has a red chief charged with a gold English lion; the main field has six wavy bars of white and blue charged with three five-pointed stars, edged in gold, representing the three main islands (Grand Cayman, Little Cayman and Cayman Brac). The crest features a turtle and a pineapple plant, and beneath the shield there is the motto HE HATH FOUNDED IT UPON THE SEAS.

Cayman Islands

GREENLAND
Danish autonomous province
The Danish flag is used.

GUADELOUPE
French overseas department
The French flag is used.

MARTINIQUE
French overseas department
The light blue flag is divided by a white cross into four parts, each of these featuring an erect white snake in the shape of the letter L. This is the initial of the name St Lucia and at the end of the 18th century, when this flag was created, the island of St Lucia was part of the then French colony of St Lucia-Martinique. The flag corresponds to the shield in the arms of this colony and in the present coat of arms of Martinique; it is flown in the island together with the French flag, although it has no official status.

MONTSERRAT
British dependent territory
Since 1960 the British Blue Ensign with the badge of Montserrat in the fly has been used. The badge consists of a shield with a female figure dressed in green embracing a black cross and supporting a golden harp. These arms date from 1909.

Montserrat

PUERTO RICO
Associated state of the USA
The flag consists of three red horizontal stripes alternating with two white ones; in addition, a blue isosceles triangle bearing a white five-pointed star is placed in the hoist. This is a variation on the Cuban flag (in 1895 the Puerto Ricans fought alongside the Cubans for independence from the Spaniards) and also recalls the American flag. The Puerto Rican flag was created in 1895 and its use was permitted in 1916.

Since 1952, when the island became an associated state of the USA, the flag has been the official flag of Puerto Rico; nevertheless, it may only be hoisted beside the American flag.

ST PIERRE AND MIQUELON
French overseas department
The flag is blue with an illustration in yellow of the three-masted sailing ship in which the French explorer Jacques Cartier landed on the island in 1535. The Basque flag (red with a green saltire and a white St George's cross) is depicted in a vertical stripe in the hoist; beneath it there is the canton from the flag of Brittany (all ermine), and lower still there is the Norman flag (red with two golden leopards). These represent nations from which other early explorers also landed in these islands. The flag is used by the local offices and organizations but has no official status.

TURKS AND CAICOS ISLANDS
British dependent territory
The British Blue Ensign with the local badge in the fly is used. The badge consists of a gold shield charged with a queen conch shell, a spiny lobster and a Turk's-head cactus, all of which are found locally. The flag was introduced in 1968.

Turks and Caicos Islands

THE VIRGIN ISLANDS OF THE UNITED STATES
Territory of the USA
The flag is white and displays the eagle from the American arms in yellow. The breast of the eagle is charged with the American shield and the claws grasp an olive branch and three blue arrows. The eagle is flanked by the letters V and I in blue, which stand for the Virgin Islands. The flag dates from 1921.

SOUTH AMERICA

ARGENTINA (2:3)

BOLIVIA (2:3)

BRAZIL (7:10)

CHILE (2:3)

COLOMBIA (2:3)

ECUADOR (1:2)

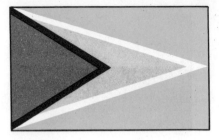

GUYANA(3:5)

PARAGUAY(1:2)

PERU (2:3)

SURINAM (2:3)

TRINIDAD AND TOBAGO (3:5)

URUGUAY (2:3)

VENEZUELA (2:3)

Falkland Islands (1:2)

Netherlands Antilles (2:3)

SOUTH AMERICA

ARGENTINA
Federal republic
The state flag consists of three horizontal stripes — sky blue, white and sky blue. In the centre, as a sign of freedom, there is the yellow "Sun of May" with thirty-two rays (alternately straight and wavy) which shone through the clouds during the first big demonstration on 25 May 1810 in Buenos Aires, when the demand was made for independence from the Spanish viceroy. The bicoloured flag was designed by General Manuel Belgrano in 1812 and was based on a cockade which had been part of the uniform of the liberation movement in 1810. (This was the Patricios regiment of Buenos Aires which had repulsed the British intervention forces in 1807.) This flag was accepted when the country gained independence in 1816, and the Sun of May was added in 1818. The Argentinian flag influenced the flag of the United Provinces of Central America, and it has been taken up by the federation's member-countries (Costa Rica, El Salvador, Guatemala, Honduras and Nicaragua), and also by Uruguay.

BOLIVIA
Republic
The three horizontal stripes of the Bolivian flag — red, yellow and green — respectively symbolize the gallantry of Bolivian soldiers, the country's mineral wealth, and the fertility of the land. The red and yellow stripes are certainly derived from the colours of Colombia and her liberator Simón Bolívar, who also liberated Bolivia (called Upper Peru between 1776 and 1825), which was named after him. The Bolivian coat of arms of 1888 is placed in the middle of the state flag. The arms consist of an oval shield depicting a landscape with a stylized illustration of Mount Potosí in bright sunshine and, in the foreground, a South American alpaca, a breadfruit tree, and a wheat sheaf, with a forest and a house in the middle distance. The upper golden border of the oval bears the name of the country BOLIVIA in red letters, and the lower blue border is charged with nine gold five-pointed stars representing the departments of the country. (Another department, Litoral, is in the process of being claimed so that Bolivia will have access to the sea.) Behind the oval there are two crossed cannon barrels, six Bolivian flags, four rifles, a Phrygian cap of liberty, an Inca battle-axe and a laurel wreath; perched on the oval shield is an Andean condor. The flag with its present order of stripes was introduced in 1851 but a number of variations had been used since Bolivia gained independence in 1825.

BRAZIL
Federal republic
The green field of the flag bears a yellow diamond charged with a blue disc representing the Southern sky with twenty-three stars. A white band

with the motto ORDEM E PROGRESSO ("Order and Progress") is placed across the disc which suggests the armillary sphere in the arms of Portugal. Green stands for the vegetation, yellow for the mineral wealth (especially the finds of gold in colonial times), and white and blue (the historic colours of Portugal) for the ancestors of the present inhabitants, who discovered and populated the country. The inclusion of the diamond on the flag recalls the regimental colours of the French military units in the early 19th century. The disc is a reminder of the arms given by King João II to Prince Manuel for his achievements during his voyages between 1495 and 1521, and until 1889 the place of the disc was taken by the coat of arms of the Brazilian Empire. The sky scene is an accurate depiction, although reversed, of twenty-three stars (in five different sizes) visible from Rio de Janeiro. The stars represent the twenty-two states and the federal district of the Brazilian Federation. The Southern Cross constellation in the centre commemorates the struggle of the Brazilian people for freedom, and the white band with the motto is a symbolic expression of the constant growth of the country. The basic pattern of the flag dates from 1822, and the most recent amendment (the addition of the last star) was made in 1968.

Brazil

CHILE
Republic
The flag of Chile has two horizontal stripes, white over red, and a blue square canton charged with a white five-pointed star in the hoist. Red stands for the blood shed for the country's freedom, white for the snow-covered Andes, and blue for the vault of the heavens above the whole country. The white star, which had been used by Chilean Indians of long ago, stands for the progress and honour of the nation; its five points are sometimes said to correspond to the five original provinces of the country. The flag was created during the struggle for Chile's liberation in 1817, and is really a simplified version of the flag of the USA with identical colours.

COLOMBIA
Republic

The flag consists of three horizontal stripes — yellow, blue and red (their proportions being 2 : 1 : 1). It was derived from the flag designed by Francisco de Miranda in 1806 and used by Simón Bolívar, and also from the colours of the former state of Great Colombia (1819 – 30) which comprised New Granada (the present Colombia with Panama), Venezuela and (from 1822) Ecuador, after Bolívar had liberated them from Spanish rule. A corresponding interpretation was that golden America was separated by the blue waters of the ocean from bloody Spain (red and yellow being Spanish colours). Sometimes yellow is taken to refer to the people of Colombia, blue to the ocean separating the country from Spain, and red to the blood shed for the country's freedom. According to the most recent interpretation yellow stands for the independence of the country, blue for gallantry, nobility and loyalty, and red for the patriots' blood shed for freedom. These colours are also used by Ecuador and Venezuela. A flag in these colours was created in 1813 (only three years after the declaration of independence).

ECUADOR
Republic

As one of the members of the former state of Great Colombia (1819 – 30) which it joined in 1822, Ecuador uses a flag with horizontal stripes of yellow, blue and red (with the proportions 2 : 1 : 1) after the pattern designed by Francisco de Miranda in 1806 and used by Simón Bolívar. In order to distinguish it from the contemporary Colombian flag, the 1845 coat of arms of Ecuador was placed in the centre of the state flag. This emblem is an oval shield showing a landscape in natural colours with a stretch of sea and a steamship carrying the rod of Mercury, a green coastline, and in the background the snow-capped volcano Chimborazo. The sun of liberty shines in the blue sky and is placed in the centre of an arc which bears the signs of the zodiac (Aries, Taurus, Gemini and Cancer) under which free Ecuador was born in the 1845 revolution. The ship commemorates the construction in Ecuador of the first steamship on the entire west coast of South America; it is also a symbol of seafaring and commerce, which is stressed by the rod of Mercury. Behind the shield there are two pairs of Ecuadorian flags and a wreath of laurel and palm. Beneath the shield there are "fasces"(as a symbol of the republican form of government), while an Andean condor (as a symbol of strength) perches on top of it. Yellow represents the richness of the country, the sunshine and the fields of wheat; blue stands for the sky, the waters of the ocean and of the rivers; and red is for the blood of the martyrs for freedom. The flag was used in the periods 1806 – 9 and 1822 – 45, and has now been in use since 1860. It was officially confirmed in 1900.

GUYANA
Republic within the British Commonwealth
The basic colour of the flag is green, symbolizing agriculture and the forests of the country. Overlaying the green there is the so-called "Golden Arrowhead", edged in white and pointing towards the fly; it represents the mineral wealth and the golden future of the country. Also based on the hoist there is a red triangle edged in black, which stands for the enthusiasm and dynamism of the people engaged in the nation-building process. The white border is for the country's water resources, and the black one is for perseverance in developing the nation, and for the endurance that will sustain the golden arrow's thrust into the future. In this complex flag, green occupies exactly 50 per cent of the area, yellow 24 per cent, red 16 per cent, white 6 per cent, and black 4 per cent. The flag is based on a design made in 1966 by the foremost American vexillologist, Dr Whitney Smith.

PARAGUAY
Republic
The present Paraguayan flag dates from 1842, when it replaced the tricolour of 1812 which was introduced by one of the first presidents of Paraguay, Dr José Gaspar Rodríguez de Francia, who was a great admirer of France and gave the flag the French colours. It has three horizontal stripes — red, white and blue. In the centre of the white stripe on the obverse side of the flag there is the state coat of arms, while the reverse side bears the Treasury seal. This is the only instance of a national flag having different designs on the obverse and reverse. Red stands for bravery, courage, patriotism, equality of rights and justice; white signifies the immaculateness of ideals, purity, peace, unity and steadfastness; and blue is for gentleness, kindness and realism. The circular coat of arms displays a wreath of olive and palm branches (representing peace and honour) embracing a golden radiant "May Star" which shone above Asunción during the memorable night of 14/15 May 1811 when the independence of Paraguay was proclaimed. On the reverse side of the flag the seal shows the motto PAZ Y JUSTI-CIA ("Peace and Justice"), and a lion guarding the Phrygian cap of liberty, the traditional symbol of freed slaves. Both emblems have, in addition, a circular inscription REPUBLICA DEL PARAGUAY.

PERU
Republic
The state flag consists of three vertical stripes — red, white and red; in the centre there is the shield from the coat of arms of 1825 which is framed by two green branches, one of laurel and one of palm, bound at the bottom with a red ribbon. The first section of the shield has a blue field charged with a golden llama (representing the country's fauna); the second has a white field charged with a green cinchona

179

tree (standing for the flora); and in the red base there is a golden cornucopia pouring out gold coins (symbolizing the mineral wealth). Above the shield there is a green laurel wreath in honour of the capital, Lima, bound with a red ribbon. (The complete armorial achievement including two pairs of crossed flags behind the shield appears on the naval ensign.) Red symbolizes the blood of those who fought for freedom, and white stands for justice and peace. The flag was introduced in 1825. Its designer, Captain General José de San Martin, was inspired in 1820 by a number of flamingoes in flight, which he considered to be a good omen, and he then designed a flag in red and white for his Peruvian Legion.

SURINAM
Republic
The flag of Surinam consists of five horizontal stripes − green, white, red, white and green − with the proportions 2 : 1 : 4 : 1 : 2. In the middle of the red stripe there is a yellow five-pointed star with a diameter equal to one-third of the flag's width. Green is the symbol of the country's fields and forests, varied resources and hope for the new Surinam, and white is for justice and freedom. Red signifies the love which urges the people to act, as well as progress and the desire to perform deeds which help to build the state. Yellow signifies self-sacrifice for unity, love of humanity, self-confidence and orientation towards the golden future of Surinam. The five-pointed star is for unity between the nation's five ethnic groups. The flag was introduced in 1975.

TRINIDAD AND TOBAGO
Republic within the British Commonwealth
The flag is red with a black diagonal stripe bordered by two narrow white stripes. Black stands for the inhabitants, their strength and unity, and also for the country's wealth. White represents the waves of the sea surrounding the islands, and it also stands for purity of ideals and for equality of all people under the sun. Red denotes the vitality of the country, the warmth and energy of the sun, and the peacefulness and courage of the people. The flag was created in 1962.

URUGUAY
Republic
According to a decree of 1830 the flag consists of four blue horizontal stripes on a white field, i.e. of nine horizontal stripes of equal width, alternately white and blue; their number recalls the nine original departments of Uruguay. A white square canton, equal in width to five stripes, bears the popular South American yellow "Sun of May"; this is a symbol of freedom and has sixteen alternately straight and wavy rays which are yellow with a black outline. The flag of Uruguay was inspired by the blue and white flag of Argentina (which waged war on Brazil for

the independence of Uruguay in 1825–8) but the strong influence of the American flag on its design can also clearly be seen. The flag has been used in its present form (except for variations in the drawing of the sun) since 1830 but the flag of 1828, with its nine blue stripes, had a similar appearance.

VENEZUELA
Republic
Venezuela's flag consists of three equal horizontal stripes coloured yellow, blue and red, and is derived from the flag of Simón Bolívar and from the colours of the former state of Great Colombia (1819–30) to which Venezuela belonged, together with Colombia and Ecuador. In the centre of the blue stripe there are seven white five-pointed stars with vertical axes and arranged in an arc, commemorating the seven provinces which in 1811 originally formed the Venezuelan Confederation. The stars have appeared on the flag since 1817 in a number of different groupings, the present arrangement dating from 1859. In the upper hoist of the state flag, in the yellow stripe, there is the Venezuelan state coat of arms of 1930, most recently amended in 1954 when the title in the arms was altered. Its shield is divided into three sections. The first displays a golden wheatsheaf on a red field; the second has a gold field charged with three crossed Venezuelan flags and two sabres; and in the base, which is blue, there is a white horse galloping to the observer's right on a grassy ground (representing the "llanos"or plains). The shield is framed by branches of laurel and palm bound at the bottom with a ribbon in the national colours, which is inscribed 19 DE ABRIL DE 1810 – INDEPENDENCIA; 20 DE FEBRERO DE 1859 – FEDERACION; REPUBLICA DE VENEZUELA. On top of the shield there are two cornucopias. The flag dates from 1806 when it was hoisted by the leader of the liberation movement, Francisco de Miranda; in 1811 it became the flag of the Confederation of Venezuela, during 1819–30 the flag of Great Colombia, and in 1830 the flag of independent Venezuela. It was officially confirmed in 1954. Yellow signifies new opportunities and possibilities for America after liberation; red stands for Spain; and blue represents the waters of the Atlantic Ocean which separates the two countries.

FALKLAND ISLANDS
British dependent territory

The British Blue Ensign with the colony's badge of 1948, placed on a white disc in the fly, is used. The shield of the arms is divided by a wavy line. In the upper blue field there is a hornless ram standing on the tussac grass, all in natural colours — sheep-breeding forms the basis of the islands' economy — and the lower white part is charged with two blue wavy bars superimposed with the three-masted ship "Desire" whose crew discovered the islands in 1592. The ship's name is included in the motto written on the scroll below the shield: DESIRE THE RIGHT.

Falkland Islands

FRENCH GUIANA
French overseas department

The French flag is used.

NETHERLANDS ANTILLES
Co-equal dominion of the Dutch crown

The flag is white with a red vertical stripe passing beneath a blue horizontal stripe in the centre of which there are six white five-pointed stars, elliptically arranged. The colours are those of the Dutch flag, and the stars represent the six main islands of the Netherlands Antilles. The flag was introduced in 1959.

AUSTRALIA AND OCEANIA

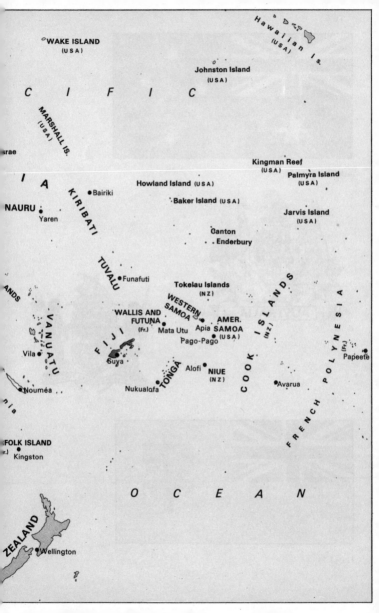

AUSTRALIA (1:2)

FIJI (1:2)

KIRIBATI (1:2)

NAURU (1:2)

NEW ZEALAND (1:2)

PAPUA-NEW GUINEA (3:4)

TO·LEAD·IS·TO·SERVE

SOLOMON ISLANDS (2:3)

TONGA (1:2)

TUVALU (1:2)

VANUATU (3:5)

WESTERN SAMOA (1:2)

American Samoa (1:2)

Cook Islands (1:2)

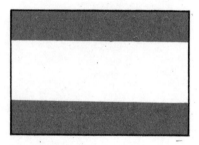

French Polynesia (2:3)

Guam (21:40)

Marshall Islands (1:2)

Micronesia (3:5)

Niue (1:2)

Norfolk Island (1:2)

Northern Marianas (20:39)

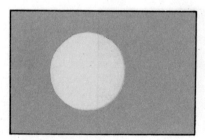

Palau (5:8)

Pitcairn Islands (1:2)

Wake Island (2:3)

Wallis and Futuna (10:13)

AUSTRALIA AND OCEANIA

AUSTRALIA
Independent state within the British Commonwealth
The Australian national flag comprises the British Blue Ensign bearing in the fly, instead of a badge, four white seven-pointed stars and one smaller five-pointed star arranged in the form of the constellation of the Southern Cross (1 + 2 + 1 + 1): the names of the stars are Gamma Crucis, Beta Crucis, Delta Crucis, Epsilon Crucis and Alpha Crucis. Under the canton, which contains the British Union Flag, there is a large white seven-pointed star called the "Commonwealth Star", representing Australia with her seven divisions (six states and one territory). Until 1909 this star had only six points. The Union Flag recalls the historical and political ties between Australia and the United Kingdom. The flag was created in 1901 but did not receive the Royal Assent until 1954. As her merchant flag, Australia uses the British Red Ensign with the same arrangement of stars as on the national flag. The Australian flag is also flown in the Ashmore and Cartier Islands, the Australian Antarctic Territory, Heard and MacDonald Islands, the Cocos Islands, the Macquarie Islands, the Coral Sea Islands, and in Norfolk Island which also has a local flag.

Australia

Fiji

FIJI
Independent state within the British Commonwealth
The current flag of independent Fiji is a modification of the old British colonial service flag, now in light blue (in order to differentiate it from the flags of Australia and New Zealand) with the shield from the Fijian coat of arms of 1908 in the fly. The red chief displays a golden lion of England holding a brown cocoa pod; the main part of the shield is white divided by a red cross into four quarters, the first one charged with green sugar-cane stalks, the second with a coconut palm, the third with a white dove carrying a green olive twig in its beak and the fourth with a yellow bunch of bananas. The upper edge of the

horizontal branch of the cross lies on the middle of the flag's width. The flag was introduced in 1970.

KIRIBATI
Republic within the British Commonwealth
The flag of Kiribati has a typically heraldic character and is based on the state coat of arms. The upper part is red, while the lower part is divided into six wavy stripes, alternately white and blue. A yellow sun with nine straight and eight wavy rays rises from the sea, surmounted by a yellow frigate bird in flight. The flag was introduced in 1979, replacing the British blue service flag with the badge of the Gilbert and Ellice Islands in the fly.

NAURU
Republic with special status within the British Commonwealth
The flag is dark blue with a narrow yellow horizontal stripe (one-twelfth of the width) in the middle and a white twelve-pointed star in the bottom left. Blue represents the waters of the Pacific Ocean in which Nauru lies. The yellow stripe symbolizes the Equator while the position of the star indicates the geographical position of the island which is situated only one degree south of the Equator. The twelve points of the star stand for the island's twelve original tribes. The flag was introduced in 1968.

NEW ZEALAND
Independent state within the British Commonwealth
The flag of New Zealand comprises the British Blue Ensign bearing in the fly, instead of the usual badge, four red five-pointed stars edged in white and arranged in the form of the constellation of the Southern Cross. The stars are of unequal size. The flag was introduced in 1869 (for the use of government ships) and its present shape was approved in 1902. The merchant flag is like the British Red Ensign with the four stars of the Southern Cross in the fly, this time all white. The New Zealand flag is also used in the country's dependencies, namely, Tokelau Islands and Ross Dependency.

PAPUA NEW GUINEA
Independent state within the British Commonwealth
The flag is divided into two triangular fields: black (in the hoist) and red (in the fly). The black field is charged with five white five-pointed stars (one smaller than the others) arranged in the form of the constellation of the Southern Cross, as in the Australian flag. The red field bears a stylized design of a yellow bird of paradise — the country's national symbol — in full flight. The Southern Cross is a reminder that the country belongs to the Southern Hemisphere, and the bird of paradise stands for freedom and unity. Red and black are traditional colours in native art and have no special symbolism. The flag was introduced in 1971.

SOLOMON ISLANDS
Independent state within the British Commonwealth
The flag is divided by a yellow diagonal (its width equalling one-eleventh of the flag's width) into two fields, the upper one being blue and the lower one dark green. In the hoist of the blue field there are five white five-pointed stars (2 + 1 + 2) representing the five administrative divisions of the country: Eastern, Western, Malaita, Central and Eastern Outer Islands District. Yellow stands for the sun, blue for the waters of the Pacific Ocean, and green for the fertile land. The flag was officially introduced in 1977 when it replaced the British Blue Ensign with the shield from the arms within a white disc in the fly.

TONGA
Independent realm within the British Commonwealth
The flag is red with a white canton which contains a red couped cross taken from the state coat of arms of 1862. The cross is Tonga's national symbol and indicates that the people of the islands are Christians, red representing the colour of Christ's blood. Originally the flag of Tonga was white with a red cross in the centre but in 1863 it was altered in order to avoid confusion with the flag of the International Red Cross. The model for this change — the British merchant Red Ensign — is unmistakable.

TUVALU
Independent state within the British Commonwealth
The flag retains the pattern of the British Blue Ensign but its colour is light blue (as in the Fijian flag). The British Union Flag is borne in the canton and in the fly there are nine yellow five-pointed stars (five of them pointing downwards); their pattern reflects the geographical position of each island, assuming North to be in the hoist. The islands are — from the North — Nanumea, Nanumanga, Niutao, Nui, Vaitupu, Nukufetau, Funafuti, Nukulailai and Nurakita; the last-mentioned is uninhabited except during the coconut harvest. The flag was introduced in 1978 at the time of the country's declaration of independence, replacing the short-lived Blue Ensign with a white disc bearing the shield from the Tuvalu state coat of arms.

VANUATU
Republic within the British Commonwealth
The flag consists of two horizontal stripes, red over green, with a black triangle based on the hoist, which extends a narrow black stripe horizontally across the flag between the red and green stripes. A yellow band is placed through the centre of the black stripe, continuing inside the triangle along two of its sides and forming a letter Y. The black triangle bears the emblem from the state coat of arms — a yellow curved boar's tusk with two yellow crossed"namele"ferns. The red stripe sym-

bolizes – according to a local tradition – the blood of sacrificial pigs, but it also stands for the human blood which unites all the inhabitants of the country. The green stripe represents the Vanuatu islands, while black stands for the fertile soil and for the Melanesian population. The yellow Y-shaped stripe symbolizes peace within the islands, which form a letter Y. The yellow boar's tusk, a favourite ornament of the natives, represents power and riches. The two crossed "namele" ferns used to be symbols of the native chiefs, and now represent the new state and its constitution. The thirty-nine fronds of the ferns correspond to the number of members of the Representative Assembly. The flag was introduced in 1980 and has taken over the colours, if not the pattern, of the flag of the Vanuaaku Party.

WESTERN SAMOA
Monarchy (with an elected ruler) within the British Commonwealth
The flag is red with a blue canton containing five white five-pointed stars arranged in the shape of the constellation of the Southern Cross. The stars are not of equal size, and they commemorate the fact that between 1920 and 1962 Western Samoa was a trust territory of New Zealand. Red stands for courage, white for purity, and blue for freedom. The flag was introduced in 1948 but until 1949 there were only the four larger stars in the canton.

Dependent Territories

AMERICAN SAMOA
Territory of the USA
The flag is blue with a white triangle, edged in red, based on the fly. The triangle extends to the hoist and bears the American eagle in flight in proper colours and facing towards the hoist. It grasps the symbol of power of the Samoan chiefs, the "uatogi" (war-club), and the symbol of wisdom of the councils, the "fue" (ritual stick). The colours of the flag are both Samoan and American, and the American eagle, holding traditional Samoan symbols, represents the protection and friendship of the United States. The flag was introduced in 1960.

ASHMORE AND CARTIER ISLANDS
Australian overseas territory
The Australian flag is used.

BAKER ISLAND
Territory of the USA
The American flag is used.

COOK ISLANDS
Associated state of New Zealand
The British Blue Ensign with a circle of fifteen white five-pointed stars in the fly is used. White and blue are the colours of the Democratic Party. According to the official interpretation, blue stands for the Pacific Ocean, and white for the peace-loving inhabitants of the islands. The stars symbolize the main islands of the archipelago, while their equal size and the circular arrangement denote equality and interdependence of the individual members of the island community. The flag has been used since 1979, when the Democratic Party won the elections. Previously, between 1973 and 1979, a green flag with a circle of yellow stars had been used, these two colours being those of the then ruling Cook Islands Party.

CORAL SEA ISLANDS
Australian territory
The Australian flag is used.

FRENCH POLYNESIA
French overseas territory
The flag has three horizontal stripes of red, white and red (their proportions being $1:2:1$) so that it corresponds to the shield of the arms which were created in 1939 when the territory was still called French Oceania, this name being changed in 1957. Red stands for courage, and white is for both the purity of ideals and a bright future. The flag is always hoisted beside the French flag but has no official status.

GUAM
Territory of the USA
The flag is blue with a narrow red border, featuring in the centre an ellipse, also with a red border. This contains the illustration from the seal of Guam, showing the estuary of the river Agaña, a sailing boat and a coconut palm, all in natural colours. Across the seal the name of the island is inscribed in red. The flag was introduced in 1917 and was accepted by the Guam Congress in 1948; the red border was added in 1960. The flag can only be flown side by side with the American flag.

HOWLAND ISLAND
Territory of the USA
The American flag is used.

JARVIS ISLAND
Territory of the USA
The American flag is used.

JOHNSTON ISLAND
Unincorporated territory of the USA
The American flag is used.

KINGMAN REEF
Territory of the USA
The American flag is used.

MARSHALL ISLANDS
State in association with the USA
The Marshall Islands separated from the Trust Territory of the Pacific Islands on 1 May 1979 and hoisted a new flag. This is blue with two diagonal stripes of orange over white, and in the canton a white star with four long rays and twenty shorter ones. The four long rays are said to stand for the capital, Majuro, and the three administrative districts of Wotje, Kwajalein and Jaluit; the twenty short rays stand for the municipalities. The blue field stands for the Pacific Ocean, and the white ray for brightness; orange represents wealth and bravery.

MICRONESIA, FEDERATED STATES OF
Trust territory of the USA
The light blue flag bears four five-pointed stars arranged in a diamond and placed so that one of the points of each star is directed away from the centre of the circle. The number of stars corresponds to the four states of this territory: Kosrae, Ponape, Truk and Yap, and blue and white are the colours of the United Nations which has entrusted the territory to the USA. The flag was introduced in October 1978 and replaced the former flag of the Trust Territory of the Pacific Islands, which was similar except that it had six stars. The flag is flown alongside those of the UN and the USA. Each of the four states has its own flag.

MIDWAY
Unincorporated territory of the USA
The American flag is used.

NIUE
Associated state of New Zealand
The British Union Flag in the canton of a yellow flag recalls the British protectorate which was declared in the island in 1900. Yellow symbolizes the sun shining brightly above the island, and the warm feelings of the islanders towards New Zealand, which assumed the administration of Niue in 1901. The four yellow stars on the arms of the St George's cross represent — even if in a different colour and grouping — the constellation of the Southern Cross from the flag of New Zealand, while the larger yellow star on a dark blue disc in the centre of the cross is the symbol of the island of Niue. The flag was introduced in 1974.

NEW CALEDONIA
French overseas territory
The French flag is used, although a local flag is under consideration.

NORFOLK ISLAND
Australian overseas territory
The flag consists of three vertical stripes of green, white and green (in the proportions 7 : 9 : 7) and features in the middle of the white stripe a tall, symmetrical Norfolk Island pine ("Araucaria excelsa") in green. In its natural home this tree grows to a height of 60 metres (200 feet) and is therefore a monumental symbol of Norfolk Island. The flag was introduced in 1980.

NORTHERN MARIANAS
Commonwealth in association with the USA
The Northern Marianas separated from the Trust Territory of the Pacific Islands in 1976 to become a separate territory, and adopted a flag and seal of its own in the same year. The flag is blue with a device in the centre consisting of a grey "latte"stone symbolic of the ancient Chamorro culture of the islands, surmounted by a white star which stands for the commonwealth.

PALAU, REPUBLIC OF
Associated state of the USA
The Palau Islands separated from the Trust Territory of the Pacific Islands on 1 January 1981 to become an autonomous republic in association with the USA. The flag adopted on that date is light blue with a yellow disc set slightly off-centre towards the hoist. The disc represents the moon as a symbol of national unity, and the blue field signifies "the final passage of the foreign administering authority from our land". The flag was the winning entry in a competition.

PALMYRA ISLAND
Territory of the USA
The American flag is used.

PITCAIRN ISLANDS GROUP
British dependent territory
The British Blue Ensign is used with the Pitcairn coat of arms of 1969. The shield is blue with a green triangle, edged in gold, in the base. This is charged with a Bible in proper colours and a golden anchor of HMS Bounty, symbolizing the origin of the local population. The helmet on top of the shield bears the crest which consists of a wheelbarrow and a slip of miro (type of food plant), standing on a grassy mount. The crest wreath and the mantling are green and gold. The flag design was proposed in 1983.

TOKELAU ISLANDS
Island territory of New Zealand
The flag of New Zealand is used.

WAKE ISLAND
Unincorporated territory of the USA
The field of the flag consists of three sections, two horizontal — white over red — and a blue vertical section in the hoist. The right side of the blue section protrudes slightly in the form of an obtuse wedge and bears a yellow disc with WAKE ISLAND in blue letters forming a circular inscription, together with a blue outline map of the three islands of the atoll: Wake, Wilkes and Peale. These three islands are also represented by three yellow five-pointed stars in the blue field. White stands for truth, red for courage, yellow for loyalty, and blue for the waters of the Pacific Ocean. White, blue and red are also the colours of the USA. The flag has no official status.

WALLIS AND FUTUNA
French overseas territory
The flag is red with four white isosceles triangles placed in the middle; the triangles have their apexes turned towards the centre and are at right angles to each other. In the upper hoist there is a small French tricolour separated from the red field by narrow white stripes. Red symbolizes courage, and white stands for purity of ideals. The triangles signify three native kings of the islands, and the French administrator; the French tricolour is a reference to French sovereignty. Except for this addition the flag is the same as that which dates from the time of the reign of King I. P. Lavelua in the 19th century. The flag has no official status.

ANTARCTICA

The division of the Antarctic continent into sectors (ARGENTINIAN ANTARCTIC TERRITORY, AUSTRALIAN ANTARCTIC TERRITORY, BRITISH ANTARCTIC TERRITORY, CHILEAN ANTARCTIC TERRITORY, FRENCH ANTARCTIC TERRITORY, ROSS DEPENDENCY and QUEEN MAUD LAND) is not internationally recognized. The flag of the country which lays claim to each sector is used.

BOUVET ISLAND
Overseas territory of Norway
The Norwegian flag is used.

FALKLAND ISLANDS DEPENDENCIES
British dependent territory (administered from the Falkland Islands)
The Falklands flag is used.

FRENCH SOUTHERN AND ANTARCTIC TERRITORY
French overseas territory
The French flag is used.

HEARD AND MACDONALD ISLANDS
Australian overseas territory
The Australian flag is used.

MACQUARIE ISLANDS
Australian overseas territory
The Australian flag is used.

PETER I ISLAND
Norwegian overseas territory
The Norwegian flag is used.

PRINCE EDWARD AND MARION ISLANDS
South African territory
The South African flag is used.

UN (2 : 3)

ITU (2 : 3)

UPU (2 : 3)

ILO (2 : 3)

ICAO (2 : 3)

FAO (2 : 3)

UNESCO (2 : 3)

WMO (2 : 3)

WHO (2 : 3)

IMCO (2 : 3)

IAEA (2 : 3)

WIPO (2 : 3)

United Nations Organization (UN)

In the centre of a light blue field there is the white badge of the UN — a simplified map of the world between the North Pole and 60° south with all the inhabited continents shown in outline. The map is flanked by two olive branches. The UN badge, inspired by the symbol suggested in 1945 after the San Francisco conference, was approved in 1946 with some modifications. The design of the flag was defined by the resolution of the General Assembly on 20 October 1947. Blue and white are the colours of the UN, the olive branches symbolize world peace, and the map of the world shows the extent of the UN's sphere of influence.

Within the framework of the United Nations there are a number of international organizations which are associated with the United Nations. Some of them have their own flags, and all of these are based on the colours of the UN flag. The symbolism of the colours of the flags is the same as that of the UN flag.

International Telecommunications Union (ITU)

The light blue field features a white globe with a few lines of latitude and longitude, a flash of lightning in white and the letters ITU. The organization dates from 1932 when the International Telegraphic Union of 1865 merged with the International Radiotelegraphic Union of 1906. The ITU became associated with the UN in 1947 and is based in Geneva.

Universal Postal Union (UPU)

The light blue flag features the white emblem of the UPU, which consists of the globe surrounded by five female figures symbolizing the five main continents. This emblem was based on the sculpture standing in front of the organization's headquarters in Bern. The UPU was founded in 1874 and became associated with the UN in 1948.

International Labour Organization (ILO)

The light blue flag bears a white emblem which consists of a wreath of olive branches (from the badge of the UN), three segments of a cogwheel (symbols of labour) and the letters ILO. The organization was founded in 1919, and is based in Geneva. It became associated with the UN in 1946, and was the first specialized organization to do so.

International Civil Aviation Organization (ICAO)

The light blue flag bears the winged badge of the United Nations. The ICAO was founded in 1944 and is based in Montreal; it became associated with the UN in 1947.

Food and Agriculture Organization of the United Nations (FAO)

The light blue flag bears a white circular emblem showing a stylized ear of wheat, the letters FAO and the Latin motto FIAT PANIS ("Let there be bread"). The organization, founded in 1945, is based in Rome; it became associated with the UN in 1946.

United Nations Educational, Scientific and Cultural Organization (UNESCO)
The light blue flag features a white emblem representing a stylized classical building with the letters UNESCO. The organization was founded in 1945 and became associated with the UN in 1946. It is based in Paris.

World Meteorological Organization (WMO)/Organisation Météorologique Mondiale (OMM)
The flag is identical with the United Nations flag but the badge is surmounted with a compass rose and the letters OMM WMO. The organization was founded in 1878 and is based in Geneva. In 1951 it became associated with the UN.

World Health Organization (WHO)
The badge of the United Nations on the flag is superimposed with the ancient symbol of medicine, the rod of Aesculapius entwined with a yellow serpent. The headquarters of the WHO are in Geneva; the organization was founded in 1946 and became an agency of the UN in 1948.

Inter-Governmental Maritime Consultative Organization (IMCO)
The light blue flag retains the olive branches from the UN badge while the reduced map of the world is placed on two crossed anchors linked at the top by a chain. The organization is based in London; it was founded in 1948 and became associated with the UN in 1959.

International Atomic Energy Agency (IAEA)
The light blue flag features the white olive wreath from the UN badge, which frames a schematic drawing representing an atom. The agency was founded and became associated with the UN in 1957. It is based in Vienna.

World Intellectual Property Organization (WIPO)
The light blue flag bears the circular emblem of the organization in white. This emblem is a five-pointed star placed within a circle; between its points there are five symbols of human intellectual activity; a book, a cogwheel, a hand holding a pen, the top of a violin and an ear of wheat. In the centre of the star there are the letters WIPO. The organization is based in Geneva and was founded in 1967, replacing the United International Offices for Protection of Intellectual Property of 1893. It became associated with the United Nations in 1974.

VEXILLOLOGICAL ASSOCIATIONS

Fédération Internationale des
Associations Vexillologiques

Flag Society of Australia

Flag Research Center, Winchester (USA)

Societé Suisse de Vexillologie,
Zollikon

Vexilologický klub, Prague

Cumann Vexilleolaíoch na hEireann —
The Vexillological Society of Ireland

Societas Vexillologica Belgica, Bruxelles

North American Vexillological Association, Oaks

Sociedad Española de Vexillologia, Barcelona

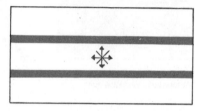

Flag Research Centre of Sri Lanka, Panadura

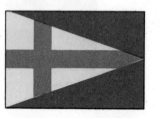

Nordisk Flagselskab (Denmark)

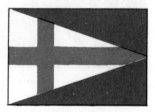

Flag Institute, Chester

Centro Italiano Studi Vessillologici, Gavirate

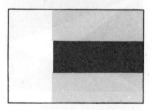

Vlaggen Documentatie Centrum Nederland, Amsterdam

GLOSSARY

ACHIEVEMENT
The whole coat of arms, including crest, supporters, motto-scroll, pavilion, and all other parts.

BAR
A horizontal stripe across a shield, one of the common charges.

BLAZON
The description of a coat of arms in heraldic language.

CANTON
On a flag — one quarter of the field, usually the upper inner quarter; on a shield — a charge consisting of a small square in the dexter chief.

CHARGE
Anything depicted on a shield as an emblem or pattern, including animals ("beasts") and geometric forms such as stripes or crosses.

CHIEF
The upper third of a shield.

CITY FLAG
A flag representing a city. This may be an armorial banner, a flag carrying a whole coat of arms or part of a coat of arms, or a simple flag of stripes.

COAT OF ARMS
Essentially, the heraldic coat of arms is a shield, or escutcheon, bearing various charges, and possibly subdivided into quarters, etc.; this is the part displayed when the shield is translated into an armorial banner. But the shield is often surrounded by other accoutrements such as crest, supporters, helm, mantling, motto, etc., and this whole achievement is often inaccurately referred to as a coat of arms.

COCKADE
A badge consisting of concentric ribbons, usually of two or more colours.

COUPED CROSS
A cross whose arms do not extend to the edges of the field, as in the flag of Switzerland.

CREST
The upper part of an achievement of arms, often placed on a helm and standing on a torse. Crest is often used, very inaccurately, as a synonym for a coat of arms.

DEXTER
The heraldic right-hand side of a shield or coat of arms (the observer's left).

EMBATTLED
Describes a dividing line on a shield similar to the battlements of a castle.

EMBLEM
A device on a flag, corresponding to a charge in a coat of arms.

ENSIGN
A flag (which can be the national flag) primarily for use at sea. Britain has three such ensigns, the Red, the White, and the Blue.

ERMINE
A heraldic colour, consisting of stylized black ermine's "tails" on a white field.

ESCUTCHEON
The heraldic name for a shield.

FIELD
The background colour of a shield or flag.

FLAGSTAFF
A mast on a ship or on land only used for flying a flag. On land it is usually a tall mast set in the ground, but it may be a smaller one that can be carried, and to which the flag is attached directly rather than made fast to halyards.

FLY
The outer part of a flag, away from the flagstaff.

GOVERNMENT FLAG
The form of the national flag used to represent the state or government authorities. Often consists of the national flag with the addition of the national arms.

GREEK CROSS
A cross of equal horizontal and vertical arms, as in the Cross of St George.

GUARDANT
Describes a heraldic beast whose head is turned to face the observer.

HALYARD
The ropes on a flagstaff to which the flag is attached, and by which it is raised and lowered.

HELM
A stylized helmet, which may have various forms, placed above a shield in a coat of arms. The torse, crest and mantling are placed on top of the helm.

HOIST
The inner part of a flag, nearest the flagstaff.

INESCUTCHEON
A small shield placed on a larger one.

INTERNATIONAL FLAG
The flag of an international organization operating on any national territory, e.g. the International Red Cross flag.

LENGTH
The horizontal dimension of a flag.

LOZENGE
A heraldic charge in the shape of a diamond, as on a playing card.

MANTLING
The slashed ribbons hanging from a crest and attached to the torse. These are usually, but not always, in the "livery" colours of a coat of arms, i.e. the colour of the field and the colour of the main charge. Often replaced by a pavilion in European heraldry.

MAST
As on a ship, but especially one from which flags are flown. Flag-masts can take various forms, but are usually thought of as taller than flagstaffs.

MERCHANT FLAG; MERCANTILE ENSIGN
The form of the national flag used by merchant shipping. In Britain it is the Red Ensign.

NATIONAL ENSIGN
Similar to the government flag, particularly when used at sea.

NATIONAL FLAG
The flag for general use representing the nation. It is the basis for the specialized flags such as the Government flag and naval ensign. In Britain it is the Union Flag, popularly referred to as the "Union Jack".

OBVERSE
The side of a flag seen when the flagstaff is on the observer's left.

PASSANT
Describes a heraldic beast depicted on all four legs and "walking" towards the dexter side of the shield, with its head in profile.

PAVILION
A mantle, usually of ermine (inside) and red (outside) placed behind a whole coat of arms (as in the Greater Arms of Denmark).

QUARTER
One quarter of a shield or armorial banner, equivalent to the canton of a flag. On a shield a quarter may be subdivided many times, as in the arms of Denmark.

RAMPANT
Describes a heraldic beast standing on two legs and reaching upwards towards the dexter chief, with its head in profile (unless it is guardant).

REVERSE
The opposite side to the obverse of a flag, i.e. the side seen when the flagstaff is on the observer's right.

ST ANDREW'S CROSS
A saltire cross of equal diagonal arms, ususally white on blue, as in the flag of Scotland.

ST GEORGE'S CROSS
A cross of equal horizontal and vertical arms, usually red on white, as in the flag of England.

SALTIRE
A cross of equal diagonal arms running from corner to corner of the flag or shield.

SCANDINAVIAN CROSS
A cross of horizontal and vertical arms, but with the vertical arms set somewhat nearer to the hoist of the flag, rather than based on the centre, as in the flag of Sweden.

SERVICE FLAG
A flag or ensign for use by government departments, either on land or at sea, or by vessels in the government service. In Britain it is the Blue Ensign, which may have the badges of the departments added in the fly.

SINISTER
The heraldic left-hand side of a shield or coat of arms, i.e. the observer's right.

STAFF
See "Flagstaff".

STATE FLAG
See "Government flag".

SUPPORTERS
Heraldic beasts which hold up a shield, and which face towards it, usually depicted as rampant, and standing on a motto-scroll. In some cases human figures are used as supporters, as in the arms of Denmark.

SWALLOW TAIL
A flag with a triangular piece cut out of the fly. These flags are often used as naval flags of command, but may be ensigns, as in the case of the naval ensign of the Federal Republic of Germany.

TORSE
The heraldic term for a crest-wreath: an elliptical band of twisted cloth placed on a helm, on which the crest stands and from which the mantling hangs. Usually in the "livery" colours of the arms, i.e. the colour of the field and the colour of the main charge.

VEXILLOLOGIST
A student of flags (from Latin vexillum, a flag).

WIDTH
The vertical dimension of a flag.

BIBLIOGRAPHY

Barraclough, E.M.C. and Crampton, W.G., **Flags of the World,** Frederick Warne, London 1981

Crampton, W.G., **The New Observer's Book of Flags,** Frederick Warne, London 1984

Crampton, W.G., **Spotter's Guide to Flags,** Usborne, London 1980

Evans, I.O., **Flags,** Hamlyn 1970

Herzog, H.-U., **Flaggen und Wappen,** VEB Bibliographisches Institut, Leipzig 1980

Inglefield, E., **Flags,** Kingfisher Books, London 1983

Ivanov, K.A., **Flags of the States of the World,** Moscow 1971

Louda, J., **Flaggen und Wappen der Welt von A – Z,** Bertelsmann, Gütersloh 1972

Neubecker, O., **Heraldry,** Macdonald and Jane's, London 1977

Pedersen, C.F., **International Flag Book,** Blandford, Poole 1971

Purves, A.A., **Flags for Ship Modellers and Marine Artists,** Conway Maritime Press, London 1983

Rabbow, A., **dtv-Lexikon politischer symbole A-Z,** Munich 1970

Smith, W., **Flags and Arms across the World,** Cassell, London 1980

Smith, W., **Flags through the Ages and across the World,** McGraw-Hill, New York 1975

Smith, W., **The Flag Book of the United States,** Morrow & Co, New York 1975

Talocci, M., **Guide to the Flags of the World,** Sidgwick and Jackson, London 1982

Wise, T., **Military Flags of the World, 1618 – 1900,** Blandford, Poole 1977

FLAG CHARTS

Flags of All Nations, Brown, Son & Ferguson, Glasgow 1981

Flags of Australia, Standard Publishing House Pty Ltd, Rozelle, NSW 1983

Flags of the United Nations, UN, New York 1980

The National Flags of the World, IBC Publications, San Francisco 1983

United States of America, IBC Publications, San Francisco 1983

The World of the Flags, John Bartholemew & Son, Edinburgh 1981

PERIODICALS

Banderas, Sociedad Española de Vexilogia, Barcelona, Spain (from 1979)

Crux Australis, Flag Society of Australia, Oakleigh, Victoria, Australia (from 1983)

The Flag Bulletin, Flag Research Centre, Winchester, Mass., USA (from 1961)

Flaggenmitteilungen, Liestal, Switzerland (from 1975)

Flagmaster, The Flag Institute, Chester, UK (from 1971)

Irish Vexillology Newsletter, Vexillological Society of Ireland, Blackrock, Dublin, Ireland (from 1984)

NAVA News, North American Vexillogical Association, Salem, Mass., USA (from 1967)

Nordisk Flaggskrift, Nordisk Flagselskab, Aalsgaarde, Denmark (from 1975)

Vexilla Belgica, Societas Vexillogica Belgica, Brussels, Belgium (from 1977)

Vexilla Helvetica, Société Suisse de Vexillologie, Zollikon, Switzerland (from 1969)

Vexilla Italica, Centro Italiano di Studi Vessillologici, Gavirate (VA), Italy (from 1974)

Vexilla Nostra, Nederlandse Vereniging voor Vlaggenkunde, Dordrecht, Netherlands (from 1966)

Vexillinfo, Societas Belgica Vexillogica, Brussels, Belgium, (from 1980)

Vexilologie, Vexillology Club of Czechoslovakia, Prague (from 1972)

Vlaggen, A. Jansen, The Hague, Netherlands (from 1979)

INDEX OF COUNTRIES

Figures in heavy type refer to illustrations

218